THE HEARTY BOYS COOKBOOK

Talk with your mouth Full

DAN SMITH and **STEVE McDONAGH**

Photographs by **LAURIE PROFFITT**

SURREY BOOKS • AN IMPRINT OF AGATE • CHICAGO

contents

Introduction   6

Dear Reader   9

Passed Hors d'Oeuvres   10

Buffet Hors d'Oeuvres   44

Starters   70

Main Dishes   90

Side Dishes   126

Desserts   150

Libations   170

Sample Menus with Timelines   202

Liquor Buying Guide   210

Acknowledgments   216

Conversion Chart   217

Index   218

introduction

Why do you insist on talking with you mouth full?" the E-mail read. "Please stop it, and please tell your directors, and the directors, producers, and hosts of other TV shows to stop teaching children that using bad manners is okay, because it just isn't." It was our first week on Food Network, and we had already angered the masses.

Well, we knew that talking with your mouth full wasn't exactly polite. We like to think that our mothers brought us up right and taught us well . . . but they didn't teach us about "TV bites": When the stage manager silently holds up both hands and begins to count backwards from ten on his fingers, your job is to garnish that platter, get the food attractively onto your dinner plate, cut yourself a (small) bite, chew properly, panic that there is dead air while you chew, swallow the food, make a yummy face, and describe the taste before your stage manager runs out of fingers.

So, this was another lesson learned the hard way, which seems to be the way we like to do things. You see, neither of us went to culinary school. We started out in New York as actors trying to pay our bills, which meant, quite simply, rolling up our sleeves and working in all aspects of the food business.

We learned how to set up outdoor bars and buffets at the U.S. Open; how to set an exquisite formal table at the French Embassy; and, when we worked luncheons at the United Nations, we became versed in treating guests royally . . . literally. We discovered valuable time-saving strategies once we started our own catering business; just the two of us cooking for groups of more than a hundred. We learned how to transport a wedding cake over thirty miles of unpaved road in rural Maine. And, while we frantically searched for undelivered tables, chairs, and china thirty minutes before a wedding ceremony began, you'd better believe we mastered the art of presenting a calm demeanor.

We soaked up all sorts of knowledge along the way and these experiences helped us become what we like to call "accidental experts." But it's important to note that although we drove along the same highway to get here, we have different views of the trip.

DAN:

Food has played a major role in my life from my earliest memories. We lived with my Italian grandparents starting when I was a year old. They lived on the first floor; we lived on the second. From the time I was able to negotiate stairs, I ate six meals a day—I'd start with breakfast with my brothers, then when they went off to school, I'd go down and sit at my grandmother's huge kitchen table, where she'd feed me Biscotti Regina and coffee milk. Then it was back upstairs for lunch and back downstairs for a second lunch. My favorite was pastina—tiny bits of pasta stirred together with butter and sharp, salty Locatelli Romano cheese. Then I'd hang around and watch my grandmother prepare any number of dishes—it always depended on the day. She'd start to make bacalao on Thursday for Friday's fish dinner, homemade meat-stuffed ravioli on Saturday for Sunday's marathon six-hour dinner, and any day during the week I was usually rewarded with a piece of her Sicilian pizza. Thank God I had a high metabolism.

STEVE:

As a child, I used to wish I had a big Italian family. I longed for masses of cousins lingering over a meal, heaping bowls of steaming pasta and meatballs as big as your head. Now, as an adult, I have Dan's big Italian family . . . and of course, I find it overwhelming (although I'm still grateful for the meatballs).

As the son of British immigrants, I honestly didn't know it was even possible to make your own tomato sauce until a high school buddy boasted about his dad's rich, spicy homemade batches. The love of food and adventure were somehow hidden deep in my English DNA, and off I went to the supermarket. I didn't even have a recipe for tomato sauce; all I knew was a commercial I had seen with crumbling blocks of cheese and juicy, bouncing tomatoes. I just kept chanting the ad copy: "with imported Romano and Parmesan cheeses, farm-fresh basil, garlic, Roma tomatoes. . . ." I remember I put together a fairly decent sauce that night too!

My career choice easily paired itself with the food business, as all New York actors work in restaurants. I wish I could tell you the actual "actor as waiter"

percentage, but I can't. I can tell you that if all the actor/waiters in New York got a summer-stock job at the same time, you'd be refilling your own bread baskets quicker than you could say, "Auntie Mame."

In fact, I met Dan during a summer-stock road tour of *The Fantasticks* in 1986. When it ended I took a catering job, which surprisingly, I found I loved. Organizing room setups suited my need for structure. Looking sharp in a tuxedo while maneuvering the staff played to the hidden dictator within me. And the food—oh, the food! The beautiful little passed hors d'oeuvres tailored to each event and exquisitely presented. This whole new culinary world excited my inner kitchen explorer.

DAN:

I didn't start cooking until a couple of years after Steve started catering. I was an actor and model in New York City, where I explored the city's many cheap restaurants. Eventually fate brought me to a fabulous boutique caterer who needed help in her small kitchen. Francine Maroukian taught me a lot of cooking techniques as well as instilling in me a hunger to start my own food business.

Wanting a more secluded area in which to test out my food chops, I moved to a small resort town in Maine and opened a café. It was a wonderful life. I got to play with food and feed people my creations, and they loved it! But there was one thing I missed . . . Steve. He'd made a move to Chicago while I'd been sharpening my skills in the mountains. So after five successful years, I opted to join him there.

The Hearty Boys was born in our eight-by-eight-foot Chicago kitchen. You could stand in the middle and touch the stove, the fridge, and the collapsible countertop which we had rigged to the wall behind the back door. Every time the business line rang, we'd run to the bedroom to pick it up, trying to sound professional and not out of breath. We had a goal: We wanted to take all the knowledge we had accumulated and bring an East Coast sensibility to the Windy City. And Chicagoans were ready to listen. They started to look to us for hip, urban parties, and reporters called for tips for their upcoming entertainment articles.

Our success quickly moved us out of the apartment kitchen and into a gourmet shop in the "Boystown" neighborhood on Chicago's north side. We served an ever-changing array of foods—all of which we created on the spot each morning and some of which you'll find in this book. The Hearty Boys continued to grow happily and steadily . . . and then, in an eight-week period during the summer of 2005, we sent a tape into Food Network and beat out 10,000 entrants to become *The Next Food Network Star;* launched our own show, *Party Line with The Hearty Boys,* and opened our first restaurant, HB. Then we topped it off with the birth of our son, Nate.

Now, *Talk with Your Mouth Full* lets us use our "accidental expertise." We get to share our irreverent views of food and entertaining as we pass along accessible recipes, anecdotes from our journey, and, of course, how-to tips we've culled from our time in the trenches.

We figure that there are two kinds of cookbooks: the ones that are displayed on the coffee table and the ones that become kitchen tools. Our hope is that this book will become a dog-eared, tomato sauce-stained, well-loved resource you can count on to walk you through whatever kind of gathering you're planning. And, to remember what we did, which is to have fun while you're doing it!

dear reader . . .

There are two different voices in this book. Steve introduces each chapter with an anecdote, then Dan presents recipes, along with thoughts on each dish. Steve then finishes with practical tips.

Many see this as a prime example of how well we work together; Steve does the event planning and execution, while Dan develops the menu. In reality, it reveals how our relationship works: Steve starts off talking, Dan waits until he can fit a word in edgewise, and Steve gets the last word.

Just so you know.

passed hors d'oeuvres

Did you ever see the film *Big Night*? Stanley Tucci and Tony Shalhoub play Italian brothers who open a restaurant in 1950s Brooklyn. It is a classic foodie flick. Tony Shalhoub is a gifted chef ("Goddamn it, I should kill you! This is so fu★king good I should kill you!"), and Stanley Tucci tries to get him to reconcile his high food standards with the realities of running a business. The plot revolves around a much anticipated visit from Italian icon Louis Prima, and the brothers pour all their assets into throwing a dinner for Mr. Prima that will showcase their culinary talents and revive their failing business.

The six- or seven-course meal they organize will fill non-Italians with self-loathing over their heritage. Multiple scenes revolve around the preparation of the dinner's show stopper—a timpano. That is, layers of meats, cheeses, vegetables, and whole eggs lovingly mounded under a shell of risotto. It is an effort, and it is impressive. Just explaining this film makes me hungry all over again.

A beautiful old movie theater here in Chicago once teamed up with a local restaurant to do a *Big Night* evening. The deal was, you'd see the film and then walk across the street where the restaurant would recreate the meal with free-flowing wine. I had finally found the perfect birthday gift for Dan! I thought I'd surprise him by having about eight guests to the house for cocktails and hors d'oeuvres before the group left for the movie and dinner. I confirmed this with a group of friends and walked over to the restaurant to make our reservations.

"It's a surprise," I told the restaurant. "Please, please, do not call our house to confirm this reservation. We will definitely be here. In fact," I continued, "do you want a credit card to hold the reservation? No? Well, here, please take it anyway, because I don't want you to confirm. Can you write 'please don't call' here next to the name? Thanks."

I left work early that afternoon, came home, and started organizing. I wanted to start the evening off with some Italian-themed passed hors d'oeuvres, so I did Shrimp Tonnato (see page 30) and Glazed Apricots wrapped in Bacon (see page 20), as well as an antipasto platter with imported meats and cheeses

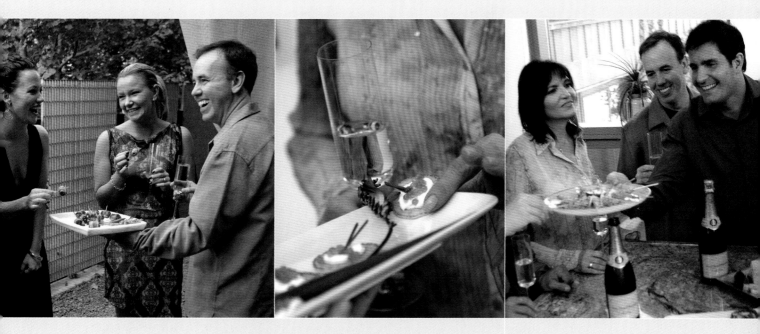

from a local Italian greengrocer. An hour before our guests arrived, I had done all my prep work, I hid my platters from Dan, stashed away all my bar needs, and all I had left to do was to take a quick shower before the guests arrived. I thought I had successfully pulled off this surprise, which, when you live and work with your partner, is no small feat.

Dan got home while I was in the shower and shouted a question into the bathroom. He wanted to know why this local Italian restaurant had left a message on the answering machine confirming our party of ten at the *Big Night* dinner that evening.

I got them back, though. As I mentioned, the wine that night was free-flowing, and I'm pretty sure I alone managed to obliterate their profit margin. My memories of the surly manager are a bit blurry, but I can attest that a truly great meal, such as this one was, celebrated with a select group of friends will always stick in your mind. My story has a great twist too: Not three weeks after the surprise dinner, I noticed that the restaurant windows were covered with banners announcing, "Coming Soon: Walgreens Drugstore."

I can't believe they went out of business and didn't even bother to call.

Garlicky Beef crostini with caramelized onion and sage whipped cream

Yield: 24 pieces
Preparation Time: 40 minutes
Cooking Time: 45 minutes

1½ pounds beef tenderloin, trimmed

2 cloves garlic, minced

1 tablespoon freshly ground black pepper

2 teaspoons kosher salt

Sage Whipped Cream, recipe follows

Caramelized Onion, recipe follows

1 recipe Herbed Crostini (see page 68)

24 small fresh sage leaves, for garnish

SPECIAL EQUIPMENT

Cooking spray for the skillet

A lot of the hors d'oeuvres that we do at The Hearty Boys are on some type of bread base, so I think it's appropriate to start with one of our tried-and-true specialties. It comes with a good story as well. A few years back, we catered a large holiday party, and this was one of the passed hors d'oeuvres. The waiters would go out with the filet, and the platters would return just as full as they'd left. I was going crazy. Why didn't they like my food? I tasted one—it was delicious. I finally asked one of our guys what he thought was the problem. He said, "Well, when we tell them it's filet of beef on crostini, they just look at us with blank faces."

I thought for a second and said, "Next time you go out, tell them it's roast beef on toast." From that point on, it was the most popular hors d'oeuvre of the night. Lesson learned? When it comes right down to it, it's really all about the taste.

Preheat the oven to 350 degrees F.

Rub the tenderloin liberally with the garlic, salt, and pepper. Spray a large skillet with cooking spray and place it over high heat for 1 minute. Put the tenderloin into the skillet and brown it on all sides, about 1 minute per side. Place it into the oven and cook until rare, 15 to 20 minutes, until the internal temperature measures 120 degrees F. Remove and let cool. Immediately before serving, slice the tenderloin thinly into about 24 pieces.

To assemble the hors d'oeuvres, place a small amount of the caramelized onions onto a crostini. Top with a rosette of tenderloin and a dollop of whipped cream. Garnish with a sage leaf and serve.

sage whipped cream

½ **cup heavy cream, chilled**
1 teaspoon ground sage
Pinch kosher salt
Pinch white pepper

SPECIAL EQUIPMENT: **Squeeze bottle**

Pour the heavy cream into a well-chilled medium-size mixing bowl. Whisk until soft peaks form. Add the sage, salt, and pepper and whisk until the peaks are firm. Spoon the whipped cream into the squeeze bottle and refrigerate until ready to use. Yield: 1 cup

caramelized onion

2 tablespoons olive oil
1 yellow onion, thinly sliced
1 tablespoon sugar
1 teaspoon kosher salt
½ **teaspoon freshly ground black pepper**

Put the oil into a medium-size skillet and place over medium heat. Add the onions and cook until translucent, about 15 minutes. Add the sugar, salt, and pepper and continue to cook slowly, stirring now and then, until the onions turn a deep golden brown. It will take about 30 minutes to get the onions to this point. Remove from the heat and let cool before storing in the refrigerator. Yield: ½ cup

MAKE AHEAD

Carmalized onion can be made 3 days in advance. Bring to room temperature before using.

staffing by the numbers

I really recommend hiring staff when you're entertaining a large group of people and want to just enjoy your party. Prices differ around the country, but waiters and bartenders average around $20 per hour, depending on your needs and the skill level of the labor. Most staffing agencies and caterers require a minimum party length of usually five hours, to secure staff.

Expect waiters and bartenders to get to your home about an hour early to set up. Have the liquors readily available so that the bartender can set up his own bar. He should keep his bar neat, his ice and beverages stocked, and your guests' drinks filled. If it's a slower event, he should be able to work the room as well. As far as the waiters are concerned, have your food, platters, and linens ready to go so they can set up the buffet, handle all the food being passed, and clear dishes, plates, glassware, and trash.

At the end of the event, the staff should leave your home looking as good as or better than they found it. Remember that it is your responsibility to tip them at the end of the night. Never allow a bartender to put a tip jar out in your home. If a guest hands him a buck, and he puts it in his pocket, fine, but soliciting tips is terribly tacky.

How many waiters or bartenders do you need? Well, for a cocktail party, we send one waiter for every 20 to 25 guests and one bartender for every 50. And keep in mind that if you pile too many responsibilities on too few staff (taking coats, answering the door, preparing supplemental foods you may have purchased), your service will suffer. What I'm getting at is this: Don't expect to get off on the cheap and hire one person to do it all. You might be disappointed to learn that those aren't superhero capes the waiters have on—they're just aprons.

petit croque monsieur

The French build their sandwiches differently from us Americans. While we pile them high with meats and cheeses, wishing we could unhinge our jaws to get our mouths around them, the French put a couple of slices of meat and one or two slices of wonderful cheese between two thin slices of excellent bread. Then, often they'll toast them so that on the outside they're crunchy and on the inside they're pure, melted goodness. Makes me wish I were in Paris again!

Lay out the bread slices on a flat work surface. Spread 3 slices liberally with mayonnaise and 3 slices thinly with mustard. Place 2 slices of ham and 1 slice of Gruyère on the mayonnaise-coated slices. Top with the mustard-coated slices.

Using the pastry brush, coat both sides of the sandwiches with melted butter. Heat a grill pan or griddle until it spits if flicked with a drop of water and toast the sandwiches until golden on both sides, 2 -3 minutes per side. Trim the crusts and cut each sandwich into 8 triangles. Serve warm.

Yield: 24 pieces
Preparation time: 10 minutes
Cooking time: 15 minutes

6 slices brioche sandwich bread (4-by-6 inches)

2 tablespoons good quality Mayonnaise, such as Hellmann's

1 tablespoon Dijon mustard

6 thin slices ham

3 slices Gruyère cheese

½ cup (1 stick) unsalted butter, melted

SPECIAL EQUIPMENT

Pastry brush

plate full of drama

You already know that "people eat with their eyes first." So the following rules of presentation are vital to a caterer's success. To look appealing, food needs some "negative" or empty space around it. Always use oversized platters. In addition, take care not to overcrowd your platter. Give your food a little room to "show off."

Avoid putting fried hors d'oeuvres directly on a solid-colored glazed plate as the oil will leave marks behind. With these types of platters, we'll use a layer of whole fresh chives or even lentils as a bed for the appetizer.

And don't forget to garnish! Whether you use a fresh peony from your garden, a tiny glittering tealight votive, or seasonal herbs tied up in twine (preferably herbs that are ingredients in the dish being served), this is one time when more drama in your life is actually good.

shaved ham on cheddar shortbread with apple jam

Yield: 24 pieces
Preparation time: 40 minutes
Cooking time: 20 minutes

2 cups all-purpose flour

12 ounces sharp Cheddar cheese, shredded (about 1½ cups)

1½ teaspoons kosher salt

1 teaspoon freshly ground black pepper

1 teaspoon sugar

½ teaspoon baking powder

Pinch cayenne

1 cup (2 sticks) unsalted butter, chilled

Sour cream

½ pound good quality ham, thinly sliced and torn into 1-by-2-inch pieces

Apple Jam, recipe follows

Flat-leaf parsley, for garnish

MAKE AHEAD

Shortbreads can be made up to 2 days in advance and stored in an airtight container.

Apple Jam can be made up to 5 days in advance.

Ham and cheese are a perfect combination. Cheddar and apples are great friends. Why not put them all together?

Put the flour, Cheddar, salt, pepper, sugar, baking powder, and cayenne into the bowl of a food processor fitted with a steel blade. Pulse a few times to combine. Cut the butter into small bits and add to the flour all at once. Pulse just until the dough begins to come together.

Transfer the dough to a floured surface and knead until all the butter is combined. Divide the dough in half and roll each piece into a log roughly 1½ to 2 inches in diameter. Refrigerate for 20 minutes.

Preheat the oven to 350 degrees F.

Slice each log into ¼-inch rounds. Place the rounds on a baking sheet and bake them in the top half of the oven for 15–20 minutes. Remove and let cool 10 minutes before transferring to a rack to cool completely.

To assemble the hors d'oeuvres, put a small dollop of sour cream onto each shortbread. Fold a piece of the ham and place it on top of the sour cream. Top with the apple jam and garnish with a parsley leaf.

apple jam

½ cup apple cider vinegar

½ cup sugar

1 Granny Smith apple, cored, peeled, and cut into ½-inch dice

¼ teaspoon allspice

Pinch kosher salt

Put the vinegar and sugar into a medium-size saucepan and bring to a boil over medium heat. Stir to dissolve the sugar, then add the apple, allspice, and salt. Cook until the consistency of jelly, about 20 minutes. Transfer to a small bowl and refrigerate until ready to use. Yield: 1 cup

skewered pork braciola with roasted tomato cream

Yield: 20–24 pieces
Preparation time: 40 minutes
Cooking time: 40 minutes

1 pound pork tenderloin, trimmed

2 cloves garlic, minced

4 ounces Romano cheese, shredded

1 tablespoon chopped fresh basil

1½ teaspoons kosher salt

2 teaspoons freshly ground pepper

Chopped fresh parsley, for garnish

Roasted Tomato Cream, recipe follows

SPECIAL EQUIPMENT

Two dozen 6-inch bamboo skewers, soaked in water for at least 1 hour

This is a riff on an old family recipe. Braciola is a traditional Italian dish of stuffed, rolled meat. My grandmother always used to pound beef or pork until it was very thin. Then she'd fill it with Locatelli Romano cheese, minced garlic, and chopped parsley. She'd tie the braciola with string, then she'd brown each piece in a big, battered skillet on her equally big, battered stove. From the skillet it would go into her saucepot, where it would simmer for hours, along with the meatballs and spicy Italian sausages that my grandfather would have stuffed earlier that day. Of course, my favorite was her braciola. It was so tender and filled with flavor that you even wanted to eat the string she'd tied it with!

Preheat the oven to 400 degrees F.

Using a sharp knife, cut the tenderloin into ½-inch medallions. Cover each piece with plastic wrap and pound to ⅛-inch thickness.

Lay the medallions out in a row and sprinkle each with garlic, cheese, basil, salt, and pepper. Roll the meat tightly around the filling and thread onto the bamboo skewers. Put the skewers on a baking sheet and place in the oven for 15 minutes.

Remove the skewers from the oven and coat each with chopped parsley. Warm the tomato cream and serve on the side in a decorative bowl.

stick it to 'em

Save your friends that awkward what-do-I-do-with-this-stick moment by passing items like the Skewered Pork Braciola with a skewer receptacle. Try half a lemon or other soft fruit placed on the platter flesh side up. Just slice the end off the fruit to give it a flat base. Thin tumblers work well too, if you put a bit of plastic wrap underneath them to keep them from slipping around. And always start off with a skewer already in your lemon or tumbler to prompt your guests. As you're passing the hors d'oeuvres, keep an eye out for guests who are stuck looking for a place to stick their stick.

roasted tomato cream

6 fresh plum tomatoes

2 cloves garlic

Olive oil

2 teaspoons kosher salt

1 teaspoon freshly ground black pepper

½ cup heavy cream

Splash dry vermouth

SPECIAL EQUIPMENT

13-by-9-inch baking dish

Preheat the oven to 450 degrees F.

Halve the plum tomatoes and place them in the baking dish. Smash and peel the garlic cloves and add to the tomatoes. Drizzle the whole with olive oil, then sprinkle with one teaspoon of the salt and the pepper.

Put the pan in the preheated oven and roast for 30 to 40 minutes, until the tomatoes are a bit charred on the bottom. Remove the tomatoes and garlic from the oven and transfer to a blender along with the pan juices. Puree, add the cream, vermouth, and remaining teaspoon of salt. Transfer to a small bowl and refrigerate until ready to serve. Yield: 1½ cups

MAKE AHEAD

Roasted Tomato Cream can be made the day before.

glazed apricots wrapped in bacon

Yield: 24 pieces
Preparation time: 25 minutes
Cooking time: 30 minutes

24 Turkish dried apricots
(see note)

1 cup white wine

2 fresh thyme sprigs

12 slices bacon, cut in half

Honey Balsamic Glaze,
recipe follows

SPECIAL EQUIPMENT

24 toothpicks

MAKE AHEAD

The apricots can be assembled
the day before and baked the
day of.

The glaze can be made up to
1 week in advance.

Anything wrapped in bacon is good. I love the sweetness and chewy texture of dried fruit paired with the salty crispness of bacon. And when the fruit is simmered in wine before being wrapped . . . well then, as my friend Karen (a true Southern belle) says, "You've just got a little piece of heaven on a toothpick."

Preheat the oven to 350 degrees F.

Put the apricots into a medium-size saucepan, along with the wine and thyme. Add enough water to just cover and place over high heat. Bring to a boil, lower the heat, and let simmer for 10 minutes. Drain the apricots and let cool. Discard the sprigs of thyme.

Wrap each apricot in a piece of bacon, secure with a toothpick, and place on a baking sheet. Bake in the top half of the oven until the bacon is crisp, about 20 minutes. Remove from the oven and let cool for 5 minutes. Drizzle with honey balsamic glaze before serving.

COOK'S NOTE: These apricots have a brighter color and milder taste than unsulfured apricots.

honey balsamic glaze

½ cup balsamic vinegar

½ cup honey

¼ cup sugar

1 teaspoon kosher salt

Combine all the ingredients, along with ¼ cup water, in a saucepan and place over high heat. Bring to a boil, lower the heat, and let simmer until reduced by half. The glaze should have a honey-like consistency. Yield: ¾ cup

Lamb-stuffed Dates wrapped in Bacon

Pitted dates are the perfect dried fruit to fill, and—once again—wrapping them in bacon doesn't hurt either! The lamb filling in this recipe is spiced with garam masala, a blend of ground spices such as cinnamon, cumin, cloves, and cardamom. It's most commonly found in Indian cuisine, and it complements both the lamb and the dates. Your guests will be pleasantly surprised by all the flavors going on in this little hors d'oeuvre.

Preheat the oven to 375 degrees F.

Enlarge the opening at one end of each date by pushing your little finger into it. Put the lamb, garam masala, parsley, salt, garlic powder, and 1½ tablespoons water into a bowl and mix well by hand. Spoon the mixture into the pastry bag. Insert the tip into the opening of each date and fill with the meat mixture.

Wrap each date in a piece of bacon and secure with a toothpick. Arrange the dates on a baking sheet and place in the top half of the oven for 5 minutes. Remove the pan and flip the dates over. Place back in the oven for another 5 minutes, or until the bacon is crisp. Remove from the oven, let cool 5 minutes, and serve.

mix 'n match

I don't feel that the foods need to necessarily "match" at a cocktail party, unless you're working within a theme. I think it's exciting to offer flavors from around the globe. After all, if your passed items are about two bites each, why can't you switch from Asian to Caribbean with just a sip of a cocktail? (Do you like how I'm working the alcohol-as-palate-cleanser motif?)

It is important, however, to think about food groups and hit all the different points of the palate. It's best to balance a mix of hot and cold hors d'oeuvres by including a chicken or beef choice, something vegetarian, a seafood option, something crunchy on a crostini, something cheesy, and maybe something spicy. Basically, you can't go wrong if you just keep an eye to variety and serve what you love!

Yield: 24 pieces
Preparation time: 30 minutes
Cooking time: 10 minutes

24 pitted dates

¼ **pound ground lamb**

1½ **teaspoons garam masala**

1 **tablespoon freshly chopped parsley**

½ **teaspoon kosher salt**

¼ **teaspoon garlic powder**

6 **bacon strips, cut into fourths**

SPECIAL EQUIPMENT

Pastry bag fitted with #32 round tip

24 **toothpicks**

MAKE AHEAD

Dates can be assembled to the point just before baking 1 week in advance and frozen. They can be baked from frozen—just increase the baking time by 2–3 minutes per side or until the bacon is crispy. Or they can be assembled the day before and refrigerated.

red curry chicken wontons with plum sauce

Yield: 50 wontons
Preparation Time: 1 hour
Cooking Time: 15 to 20 minutes

Vegetable oil

1 pound ground chicken

1 tablespoon red curry paste (see note)

8 pickled plums, pitted and chopped (see note)

1 small bunch cilantro, chopped

Square wonton wrappers

Chopped chives or chive blossoms, for garnish

Golden plum sauce or duck sauce, for serving

SPECIAL EQUIPMENT

Cup filled with water

Bread cube for testing oil temperature

MAKE AHEAD

Wontons can be assembled up to 1 week in advance and frozen. They can be cooked from frozen—just add a few minutes to their cooking time.

My nephew Jason has an ongoing love affair with Chinese buffets, which is why we found ourselves at one in Portland, Maine, last year. My whole family was there, and during dinner we noticed a group of waitresses sitting at a table making wontons. They had a little assembly line going: One woman would peel a square wonton wrapper off a large stack and put a mound of filling in the center. She'd push it down to the next woman, who moistened the wonton with water. Once again, it would get pushed down to another woman, who folded it quick as lightning into a little parcel. While I can't compete with their folding abilities, this Italian boy holds his own in the filling department!

Put the chicken, red curry paste, pickled plums, and cilantro into a medium-size bowl and mix well by hand.

Lay out 10 wonton wrappers in a row and set a cup of water nearby. Put 1 heaping teaspoon of the chicken mixture into the center of each square. Working quickly, dip your fingers into the water and moisten the edges of each wonton. Fold them over the filling to form triangles, pressing well to seal. Curl the two points of each triangle in toward each other, moisten one point, and press them together to form a bishop's hat. Repeat with the remaining wontons and filling. Place on a baking sheet and refrigerate for at least one hour.

When ready to cook, pour 3 inches of vegetable oil into a large saucepan and place over medium heat until a bread cube dropped into the oil browns within 30 seconds.

Drop the wontons into the hot oil by the dozen and cook until puffed and golden, about 3 minutes. Remove and place on a rack to let the excess oil drain. Garnish with chopped chives or chive blossoms, and serve plum sauce on the side.

COOK'S NOTE: Red curry paste is a spicy, pungent Thai condiment made with dried chiles, garlic, and lemongrass that can be found in Asian markets. Pickled plums aren't as sweet as you might expect. They're tart and a little pungent with slightly sweet notes and can be found in Asian markets.

velvety chicken liver mousse on rye with shallot confit and tangerine marmalade

Yield: 24 pieces
Preparation time: 60 minutes
Cooking time: 60 minutes

2 bay leaves

1 small bunch flat-leaf parsley, plus additional for garnish

20 black peppercorns

1 pound chicken livers

¾ cup (1½ sticks) unsalted butter

½ cup diced shallots

3 cloves garlic, chopped

½ teaspoon nutmeg

1 teaspoon dry mustard

½ teaspoon ground cumin

¼ cup brandy

1 teaspoon kosher salt

½ teaspoon ground black pepper

⅓ cup heavy cream

12 slices 2-inch-square cocktail rye, cut in half diagonally and lightly toasted

Tangerine Marmalade, recipe follows

Shallot Confit, recipe follows

I grew up on Long Island in a heavily Italian and Jewish neighborhood, so if there's one thing I know, it's chopped liver. It can be a little confusing—an Italian named Smith who's up on Jewish cuisine—but there you have it! One of the best compliments I ever received came at a party we catered for a Jewish client in Chicago. He tasted the chicken liver mousse and said to one of our waiters, "You know, this is almost as good as my grandmother's." It may not look like much in print, but if you can make chicken livers that are almost as good as someone's Jewish grandmother, you're doing all right.

Put the bay leaves, parsley, and peppercorns into a large saucepan and fill with 8 cups water. Bring to a boil, reduce the heat to low, and add the chicken livers. Simmer for about 8 minutes, until the livers are firm but still slightly pink inside.

Drain the livers and run them under cool water for 3 minutes. Discard the bay leaves, parsley, and peppercorns and set the livers aside.

Melt the butter in a large skillet. Add the shallots, garlic, nutmeg, mustard, and cumin and cook over medium-low heat for about 20 minutes, until the mixture is soft and golden.

Transfer the mixture to the bowl of a food processor and add the chicken livers. Add the brandy, salt, and pepper and process until smooth. Add the cream and pulse until combined.

Spoon the mousse into a small bowl, cover, and refrigerate until ready to use. Remove from refrigerator 1 hour before serving so that it will spread easily.

To assemble the hors d'oeuvres, spread the rye triangles with a small amount of the shallot confit. Spread about 1 teaspoon of the mousse on top of the confit and top with a dollop of marmalade. Garnish with a small parsley leaf.

tangerine marmalade

2 tangerines, pitted and finely chopped, rind and all

¾ cup sugar

¼ cup orange juice

Put all the ingredients, along with 1 cup water, into a saucepan and place over high heat. Bring to a boil, lower the heat, and let simmer for 30 minutes. The mixture will be slightly thick and syrupy. Let cool slightly and transfer to a covered container. Store in the refrigerator. Yield: 1 cup

shallot confit

7 shallots, peeled and thinly sliced

1 cup olive oil

2 teaspoons kosher salt

1 teaspoon freshly ground black pepper

Preheat the oven to 300 degrees F.

Put the ingredients into a small baking pan and cover with foil. Place in the top half of the oven for 1 hour. Remove, let cool, and store in the refrigerator until ready to use. Yield: 1 cup

MAKE AHEAD

The mousse can be made up to 2 days in advance.

The Tangerine Marmalade and the Shallot Confit can be made up to 1 week in advance.

sliced Duck and Provençal olive Tartine

Yield: 24 pieces
Preparation time: 45 minutes
Cooking time: 20 minutes

1 recipe Basic Crostini,
(see page 68)

¼ cup extra-virgin olive oil

1 bulb fresh fennel, chopped

¼ cup chopped onion

½ cup kalamata olives, pitted
and halved

½ cup Spanish olives with
pimentos, halved

1 plum tomato, diced

1 teaspoon herbes de Provence

1 teaspoon fresh grated
orange zest

¼ cup freshly squeezed
orange juice

3 tablespoons chopped
fennel fronds

Three 8-ounce duck breasts,
skin on

Kosher salt and freshly ground
black pepper to taste

24 orange supremes, for
garnish (about 2 oranges)

A *tartine* is simply a French open-faced sandwich. It can be made on any type of bread with any number of ingredients. I thought it would be fun to shrink it down to bite size and pair the richness of duck breast with the robust and sunny flavors of Provence. It also gets points for being a very elegant hors d'oeuvre!

Preheat the oven to 400 degrees F.

Pour the olive oil into a small skillet and place over medium heat. Add the fennel bulb and onion and cook, stirring occasionally, until the onion is translucent, about 10 minutes. Add both kinds of olives, the tomato, herbes de Provence, orange zest, and orange juice. Cook until the liquid is gone, about an additional 10 minutes.

Remove from the heat and pour the mixture into a food processor bowl fitted with a steel blade. Pulse until the mixture is coarsely chopped. Spoon into a small bowl and mix in 1 tablespoon of the fennel fronds. Set aside to cool.

Score the skin of the duck breasts, season them with salt and pepper, and place them in a cold ovenproof skillet skin side down. Place the pan over high heat and allow the skin to crisp. This will take about 7 minutes. Turn the breasts and sear for 1 minute. Place the pan in the oven until the breasts are medium-rare, 7 to 10 minutes. Transfer the breasts to a plate and let them come to room temperature. Slice each one crosswise into eight pieces.

To assemble, place a small mound of the olive mix onto each toast. Top with a duck slice. Garnish with an orange supreme and chopped fennel fronds.

COOK'S NOTE: The easiest way to supreme an orange is to slice both ends off and cut away the skin and pith. Be careful not to cut away too much of the flesh. Next, cut in between the membrane in order to get the segments. (Many people do this with their morning grapefruit without even knowing they're making supremes!)

MAKE AHEAD: The toasts can be made up to 1 week in advance and stored in an airtight container. The olive mix can be made the day before.

sesame chicken satay

Yield: 24 pieces
Preparation Time: 20 minutes
Cooking Time: 20 minutes

½ cup seasoned rice wine vinegar

½ cup creamy peanut butter

½ cup soy sauce

3 tablespoons sesame oil

3 tablespoons sugar

1 tablespoon freshly grated ginger

12 chicken tenders, cut in half on the bias

¼ cup chopped green onions

¼ cup chopped cilantro, plus additional for garnish

¼ cup black sesame seeds, for garnish

SPECIAL EQUIPMENT

Two dozen 6-inch bamboo skewers

MAKE AHEAD

Marinade can be made up to 1 week in advance.

This has been on our catering menu since the beginning. Being a restless cook, every so often I try to drop it from the repertoire, but our clients (and Steve) won't let me. They're right—it's delicious as an hors d'oeuvre or main dish. The creamy, tangy peanut sauce is perfect over white rice.

Preheat the oven to 350 degrees F.

Put the vinegar, peanut butter, soy sauce, sesame oil, sugar, and ginger in the bowl of a food processor fitted with a steel blade and process until well combined.

Toss the sauce with the chicken tenders and put them into a baking pan in one layer. Bake until the tenders are firm to the touch, about 20 minutes.

Let cool and thread each tender onto a skewer. Garnish with sesame seeds and green onions and serve immediately.

the nitty gritty

The two big cocktail party questions: How many different types of hors d'oeuvres should I serve, and how many pieces of each should I make?

- Five different passed hors d'oeuvres is a good variety. Too many choices can frustrate your guests as they may have long waits before a particular favorite is circulated again.
- Supplement passed hors d'oeuvres with three or four buffet choices. People can feel shy about taking too much from a waiter's tray.
- For a short, pre-meal cocktail party, expect guests to eat six to eight hors d'oeuvres in total. One "piece" generally equals one ounce, whether that's a passed item like Red Curry Chicken Wontons or a cracker spread with Bleu Cheese and Caramelized Onion Dip from the buffet.
- For a cocktail party lasting more than three hours, provide twelve to fourteen pieces per guest.

coriander Lime shrimp and mango skewers

Probably the most widely known fact about coriander is that it's the seed of the cilantro plant. Many people make the mistake of thinking that the flavor must be similar. Wrong! While cilantro has a fresh, green (and some might say soapy) taste, coriander has a warm, slightly sweet flavor with citrus undertones. We've got both flavors going on in this recipe, and I think you'll agree that they pair beautifully with shrimp and mango.

Pour the lime juice into a large mixing bowl. Add the lime zest, coriander, cilantro, green onions, sugar, salt, and pepper. Whisk to combine. Add the olive oil in a steady stream, whisking constantly.

Toss half of the vinaigrette with the shrimp and let marinate for 30 minutes. Spray the bottom of a large skillet with cooking spray and place over high heat for one minute. Working in small batches, sear the shrimp quickly. Spray the skillet with cooking spray and let it reheat before each batch for best results.

Toss the seared shrimp with the remaining vinaigrette and thread a shrimp onto each of the bamboo skewers. Cap with a mango cube. Serve immediately.

clearing house

Here is a real simple tip that people rarely think about. If you want to prepare food like a pro, you need to set your work area up the way pros do. Think of professional kitchens. Everything is kept off the flat surfaces to maximize the accessible workspace. I frequently drop by a client's house and see that they've still got all their tchotchkes on display and our chefs are struggling to prepare food around all that clutter. When you're hosting a party, your kitchen needs to be a workspace as opposed to a display area. Grab a box and pile up your cookie jars, your notepads, your toaster, your photos, and your mug full of random pens and put it all away for a few hours. You'll thank me.

Yield: 24 skewers
Preparation time: 20 minutes
Cooking time: 15 minutes

¼ cup fresh lime juice

Zest of 2 limes

1 tablespoon ground coriander

¼ cup chopped cilantro

¼ cup chopped green onions

2 teaspoons sugar

2 teaspoons kosher salt

1 teaspoon ground white pepper

1 cup olive oil

24 large shrimp peeled and deveined

Twenty-four 1-inch mango cubes (1 to 2 mangoes)

SPECIAL EQUIPMENT

Cooking spray for the skillet

Two dozen 6-inch bamboo skewers

shrimp tonnato

Yield: 24–30 pieces
Preparation time: 35 minutes
Cooking time: 4 minutes

2 tablespoons kosher salt

1 lemon, thickly sliced

4 bay leaves

1 tablespoon whole pepper-corns

1½ pounds large shrimp (16 to 20 count per pound), shell on

Tonnato, recipe follows

Capers, for garnish

Lemon zest, for garnish

MAKE AHEAD

The shrimp is best made the day of but the tonnato can be made 2 days in advance.

Shrimp is one of those foods that people just can't seem to get enough of. My cousin Steven had a shrimp bar during the cocktail hour at his wedding, and one of my aunts (who shall remain nameless) did everything but crawl up onto the buffet. I would say it was embarrassing, but it's just the way my family is—when it comes to food, it's every person for him or herself.

Put 5 quarts of water into a large pot and add the salt, lemon, bay leaves, and peppercorns. Place over high heat and bring to a boil. Add the shrimp, stir, and cook for 4 minutes. Do not overcook, or your shrimp will be rubbery.

Drain the shrimp into a colander and run under cold water. Set aside to cool, then peel and devein the shrimp, remembering to leave the tail on. Refrigerate until ready to use, but remove from the refrigerator 1 hour prior to serving (see note).

To assemble the hors d'oeuvres, butterfly the shrimp by running a knife along the outside curve of the shrimp from the head to the tail, making sure to slice almost (but not quite) all the way through. Arrange the shrimp on a platter so that the tail is standing up and place a dollop of tonnato on each one. Garnish with one caper and a pinch of lemon zest.

COOK'S NOTE: If you serve it directly from the refrigerator, the meat will be tight and not very flavorful. Do yourself a favor—take it out 1 hour before serving.

tonnato

2 cans (6 ounces each) solid light tuna in olive oil

Zest and juice of 1 lemon

2 tablespoons capers

¼ cup good-quality mayonnaise, such as Hellmann's

¼ cup extra-virgin olive oil

Freshly ground pepper to taste

Put the tuna in the bowl of a food processor. Add the lemon zest and juice, capers, mayonnaise, and olive oil and process until creamy. Stir in the pepper and place the tonnato in a decorative bowl alongside the shrimp. Yield: 1¾ cups

caprese cups

This is a great summertime hors d'oeuvre, but it's ultra important that the ingredients be the freshest and of the best quality. Toss it together right before serving, and it will be like tasting summer in a little pastry cup.

Put the tomatoes, mozzarella, and basil into a bowl. Add the olive oil, salt, and pepper and toss gently. Fill each phyllo cup with the mixture and serve immediately.

COOK'S NOTE: To make a chiffonade, stack the basil leaves on top of each other and roll them like you would a cigarette. Cut the leaves on a diagonal into thin strips and fluff to separate. Mini phyllo cups are sold in specialty food stores or the international section of upscale supermarkets.

Yield: 24–30 pieces
Preparation time: 10 minutes

⅔ cup quartered cherry tomatoes

⅔ cup fresh mozzarella, cut into ½-inch dice

⅓ cup basil chiffonade (see note)

2 tablespoons extra-virgin olive oil

½ teaspoon kosher salt

½ teaspoon freshly ground black pepper

30 mini phyllo cups (see note)

wipe that smirk off your face

Always have plenty of beverage napkins on hand for your cocktail parties. You can spend quite a bit of money on them, if you'd like, but I prefer a simple 6-inch white square. Some of the brightly colored paper napkins are coated for a glossy look, which makes them less absorbent and therefore useless for a slob like me. I also have an aesthetics issue with really bold napkins in primary colors because they tend to intensify the stains of greasy foods.

I recommend fanning your stack of napkins so that your guests can easily pick them up. If you've ever fumbled for the top napkin on a stack as a waiter stood patiently by, your fingers slipping off the top one, and making a frantic grab, and finally coming away with more than a dozen in your hand, you'll know what I mean. Place a short stack of napkins on a flat surface and place a heavy tumbler on its side atop the napkin stack. Simply press down on the glass with repeated twisting motions to rotate the napkins. It's like turning a doorknob multiple times. The first few may end up mangled, but you'll get the hang of it!

seared Ahi on wonton crisps

Ahi refers to two types of tuna: bigeye and yellowfin. Either is acceptable for this recipe—but it's important that you let your fishmonger know you need sashimi grade.

Pour 1 inch vegetable oil into a medium-size saucepan and place over medium heat. Let the oil heat for about 3 minutes. As the oil heats, cut each wonton wrapper into 4 square pieces. Very carefully drop the squares into the hot oil one at a time, working in batches of four. The wontons will bubble up and turn golden brown very quickly. Remove them with a slotted spoon to a piece of paper towel and repeat the process until all the wontons are fried.

Pour the soy sauce into a large bowl and whisk in 1 teaspoon of the ground ginger and 1 tablespoon each of the cilantro and green onion. Next, cut the tuna into 1-inch-square strips and place them in the marinade. Set aside for 15 minutes.

Place a large heavy-bottomed skillet over high heat for 3 minutes. Spray with cooking spray and immediately place the tuna strips in the pan, searing each of the four sides for 30 seconds only. Remove from the pan and set aside.

Next, place the seaweed salad in a small bowl. Add the remaining ginger, cilantro, and green onion, and the wasabi. Mix well.

To assemble the hors d'oeuvres, carefully slice the tuna strips into ¼-inch pieces. Place a small amount of the seaweed salad on a wonton crisp, top with a piece of fish, garnish with sliced green onion, and serve.

COOK'S NOTE: You can find seaweed salad in Asian markets or by the sushi in upscale supermarkets.

Yield: 24 pieces
Preparation time: 30 minutes
Cooking time: 20 minutes

Vegetable oil

6 wonton wrappers

1 cup soy sauce

2 teaspoons ground ginger

2 tablespoons chopped cilantro

2 tablespoons chopped green onion, plus additional sliced green onion for garnish

½ pound Ahi tuna

8 ounces seaweed salad (see note)

1 teaspoon wasabi powder

SPECIAL EQUIPMENT

Cooking spray for the skillet

MAKE AHEAD

The wonton crisps can be made 3 days in advance and stored in an airtight container.

smoked salmon canapés with orange butter and capers

Pictured on page 1

Yield: 24 pieces
Preparation time: 20 minutes
Cooking time: 5 minutes

1 loaf challah bread, cut into
½-inch slices

Orange Butter, recipe follows

12 ounces smoked salmon,
sliced

2 tablespoons nonpareil
capers, for garnish

Orange zest, for garnish

SPECIAL EQUIPMENT

2-inch round biscuit cutter

MAKE AHEAD

Challah toasts can be made
the day before and stored in
an airtight container.

Orange butter can be made
up to 1 week in advance.

Canapés have a long history in the world of hors d'oeuvres. In fact, Fannie Farmer devoted a section to them in a cookbook written in 1918. She writes about them being served in place of oysters at a luncheon, and how they're often served at gentlemen's dinners with a glass of sherry before the guests enter the dining room. The great thing about canapés is their versatility and the beautiful presentation that they make.

Preheat the oven to 350 degrees F.

Using the biscuit cutter, cut 24 rounds out of the bread slices and place them on a baking sheet. Toast them in the top half of the oven until lightly browned, about 5 minutes. Remove and let cool.

To assemble the hors d'oeuvres, spread the challah toasts with a little softened orange butter. Top with a small fold of smoked salmon and garnish with a few capers and a sprinkle of orange zest. Serve immediately.

orange butter

½ cup (1 stick) unsalted butter, softened

1 teaspoon orange zest

¼ teaspoon kosher salt

Pinch cayenne

Put the butter, orange zest, salt, and cayenne in a small bowl and mash together with the back of a spoon until well combined. Use right away or refrigerate for up to 1 week. Yield: ½ cup

lemon chive Blinis with sour cream and salmon Roe

Pictured on page 10

My mother, to this day, butters her pancakes and then salts them. For years we teased her mercilessly for not dousing them with pancake syrup instead. We were convinced that pancakes had to be sweet. It was especially embarrassing to go to IHOP after Sunday mass and have her act that way.

Now, blinis are, essentially, thin pancakes . . . which make perfect bases for hors d'oeuvres . . . which are usually savory. Mom, you were light years ahead of suburban Long Island. Who knew?

Combine the flour, cornmeal, sugar, baking powder, and salt in a mixing bowl. Whisk in the egg, butter, and milk until the batter is smooth. Add the chives and lemon zest and mix until combined.

Spray a 10-inch nonstick skillet with cooking spray and place over medium heat for 2 minutes. Working quickly, drop the batter into the skillet by the teaspoonful—you'll be able to fit about eight blinis. Cook until golden on the bottom, about 1 minute. Using a spatula, flip the blinis and cook an additional 30 seconds. Remove to a plate and continue until all the batter has been used. The recipe can be prepared up to this point 2 days in advance (see note).

When you are ready to assemble the canapés, top each blini with a small dollop of sour cream and a couple of salmon roe. Garnish with a piece of chive and serve.

Yield: 24 pieces
Preparation Time: 30 minutes
Cooking Time: 20 minutes

6 tablespoons all-purpose flour

6 tablespoons cornmeal

1½ teaspoons sugar

¼ teaspoon baking powder

½ teaspoon kosher salt

1 egg, lightly beaten

2 tablespoons unsalted butter, melted

⅝ cup whole milk

1 tablespoon finely chopped chives, plus some snipped chives for garnish

1½ teaspoons lemon zest

1 cup sour cream

1 jar salmon roe

MAKE AHEAD

Blinis can be made up to 2 days in advance and frozen in an airtight container with wax paper between the layers. Cook frozen in a 350 degree F oven for 2 minutes.

artichoke fritters

Yield: 24–30 fritters
Preparation Time: 35 minutes
Cooking Time: 30 minutes

Vegetable oil

One 18-ounce can artichoke hearts, drained

2 cloves garlic, minced

3 green onions, chopped

¼ cup whole milk

1 large egg, beaten

1 teaspoon lemon zest

2 teaspoons fresh lemon juice

1 cup all-purpose flour

¾ teaspoon baking powder

1 teaspoon kosher salt

½ teaspoon freshly ground black pepper

Lemon Dipping Sauce, recipe follows

MAKE AHEAD

Batter can be made the day before. Fritters are best fried day of.

Lemon dipping sauce can be made up to 3 days in advance.

Fritters are basically fried dough—it's what you add to them that makes them interesting. I like to think of these as little artichoke pillows. They're light and fluffy, and when you tear them in half, you'll see the steam rising off them and catch that mouthwatering aroma of artichoke, garlic, and tangy lemon. So stop reading already and go make a batch!

Pour 3 inches of vegetable oil into a heavy-bottomed pot and place over medium heat until a bread cube placed in the oil browns within 1 minute.

Coarsely chop the artichokes and put them in a large mixing bowl. Add the garlic and green onions, milk, egg, lemon zest, and lemon juice.

Combine the flour, baking powder, salt, and pepper in a separate bowl and quickly stir the dry ingredients into the artichoke mix. Drop the fritters by heaping teaspoonful into the hot oil and fry until golden brown, about 5 minutes. Drain on paper towels and serve immediately.

lemon dipping sauce

1 cup sour cream

Juice of 1 lemon

1 teaspoon lemon zest

1 teaspoon kosher salt

½ teaspoon sugar

Dash hot sauce

Mix all the ingredients in a small bowl. Use a small dollop on each fritter. Yield: 1 cup

cajun crab-stuffed pepperoncini

Yield: 24 pieces
Preparation Time: 30 minutes

24 pepperoncini peppers, seeded

1 pound cream cheese, at room temperature

8 ounces crab claw meat, shredded

1½ tablespoons Cajun seasoning

1 teaspoon dried thyme

1 tablespoon hot sauce

2 tablespoons chopped fresh parsley, for garnish

This was one of the first recipes that Steve crafted when we started our catering business in Chicago. While it's perfectly suited for a smaller crowd—it's fairly labor intensive—it's not a lot of fun to put together for 200 guests. Which is exactly what we had to do one weekend. Steve seeded 400 pepperoncini, and I filled them. I have to say, I had the sweeter end of the deal. By the end of the day, Steve's right hand had taken on the same hue as the pepperoncini—we still have a picture of it somewhere. It's totally worth it though—the sweetness of the crab mixed with the creaminess of the cheese pairs really well with the tang of the pepperoncini—it's a flavor party in your mouth!

Place the cream cheese in the bowl of an electric stand mixer fitted with the paddle attachment and beat until smooth. Add the crab and continue to mix. Add the Cajun seasoning, thyme, and hot sauce and mix well. Transfer the mix to a pastry bag and pipe it into the cleaned pepperoncini (see note). Refrigerate until ready to serve. Make a small mound of the chilled pepperoncini in the center of a large serving platter and sprinkle with the chopped parsley. Serve immediately.

COOK'S NOTE: A large resealable freezer bag with one corner cut off can be used instead of the pastry bag.

Fray's spinach parmesan balls

There's a controversy within the family as to whether this recipe came from my mother, for whom I've named it, or from my mother's Aunt Mary. You can be sure that when Aunt Mary gets a copy of this book, there are going to be some phone calls made, and it's going to be *the* topic of discussion at the next family gathering. I can tell you, though, that these flavor-packed balls have been a staple at our gatherings and in our catering business for years. So, Aunt Mary and Mom, you can both take credit and be proud.

Preheat the oven to 350 degrees F.

Squeeze the excess water from the spinach and place it in a large mixing bowl. Add the remaining ingredients and mix well by hand. (Wearing latex gloves while mixing and forming the balls will keep your hands from getting clumped up with spinach mix.)

Form the mixture into 1-inch balls, either by hand or by using a small ice cream scoop. Place the balls closely together on a sheet pan. Bake on the top half of the preheated oven until firm to the touch, 20 to 25 minutes. Let the spinach balls cool for 5 minutes, then remove them from the pan with a spatula and serve immediately.

COOK'S NOTE: Make sure to use margarine. We tried making these with butter once but the fat in the butter tends to leach out of the spinach balls when baking, leaving them dry, whereas the margarine combines well with the ingredients and keeps them moist.

Yield: 30–40 pieces
Preparation Time: 20 minutes
Cooking Time: 25 minutes

1-pound package frozen chopped spinach, thawed

5 eggs

1 large onion, minced

10 tablespoons margarine, melted (see note)

1 cup shredded Parmesan

2 cloves garlic, minced

½ teaspoon dried thyme

½ teaspoon cayenne

1¾ cups Italian-style bread crumbs

MAKE AHEAD

The baked spinach balls can be frozen for up to 1 week. Cook from frozen in a 350 degree F oven for 20–25 minutes.

watermelon gazpacho shooters

For a short time, we ran the restaurant at The Hotel Florence in Chicago's historic Pullman district. The clientele wasn't very adventurous, so I was always trying to sneak fun, untraditional dishes onto the lunch buffet. One hot summer day, I decided to put out this watermelon gazpacho. I filled the bottom tray of a round chafing dish with ice and set the top tray, filled with gazpacho, on top. About halfway through the lunch service, one of our new bussers came back into the kitchen and said, "Dan, someone put that soup out cold, so I lit the Sterno under it—it's getting nice and hot now." After I picked my jaw up off the floor, I hustled out to the buffet to clear the now-warm watermelon gazpacho before someone could help themselves to it.

Put the watermelon, tomatillos, jalapeño, lime juice, lime zest, salt, and cayenne into a food processor, working in batches if necessary. Process the mixture, leaving it slightly chunky. Chill well before serving, at least 1 hour and up to 1 day. To serve, pour the gazpacho into shot glasses and garnish with a lime slice.

Yield: 20–24 shooters
Preparation time: 15 minutes

4 cups diced seedless watermelon (about 3 pounds)

1 cup diced tomatillos (about 2 tomatillos)

1½ tablespoons diced jalapeño (about 1 small jalapeno, seeded)

3 tablespoons fresh lime juice

Zest of 1 lime

½ teaspoon kosher salt

Pinch cayenne

1 lime, thinly sliced, for garnish

SPECIAL EQUIPMENT

Two dozen 2-ounce shot glasses or cordial glasses

ice ice baby!

Ice sculptures no longer need to be those scary swans with interlocking necks or two hearts with your initials! We've had our local ice house sculpt everything from sushi tables to bars to the super-popular Martini Luge (the liquor is poured into a small tube that runs through the actual sculpture and into your guest's waiting glass). Just look in the yellow pages under "ice." You'll find most ice houses are eager to take your creative input and do custom carvings. These are perfect for Lemon Drop shots, passing sweet after-dinner liqueurs, and oyster shooters. If you would rather make them yourself, I've found the molds are readily available online and run about a buck apiece.

MAKE AHEAD

The shooters can be made 1 day before.

Falafel in Lettuce cups with Garlic Tahini sauce

Yield: 20–24 pieces
Preparation time: 20 minutes
Cooking time: 15 minutes

2 heads Boston lettuce

One 15-ounce can chickpeas

2 cloves garlic, crushed

¼ cup diced onion

½ cup chopped fresh parsley

½ teaspoon kosher salt

½ teaspoon ground cumin

½ teaspoon crushed red pepper

½ teaspoon dried mint

1 tablespoon tahini

1 teaspoon fresh lemon juice

1 teaspoon baking powder

3 tablespoons all-purpose flour

2 cups vegetable oil

Garlic Tahini Sauce, recipe follows

Fresh mint leaves, for garnish

MAKE AHEAD

Garlic Tahini Sauce can be made up to 1 week in advance.

Falafel is fast food—in both the Middle East and more recently, here. When Steve and I lived in New York, we would often stop and pick up falafel on our way to or from auditions. It is delicious and—bonus!—cheap. What could be better for a starving actor? Now that I'm no longer starving, I still love a good falafel.

Preheat the oven to 200 degrees F.

Break the heads of lettuce apart to use as cups for the falafel. The smaller leaves can be left whole. If some of the leaves are too large, tear or cut them in half. Cover the lettuce cups with a damp paper towel and refrigerate.

Put the chickpeas, garlic, onion, parsley, salt, cumin, red pepper, mint, tahini, and lemon juice into the bowl of a food processor and pulse until it forms a rough paste. Add the baking powder and flour and pulse until well combined.

Pour the oil into a skillet and place over medium-high heat for 2 to 3 minutes. Carefully drop the falafel into the hot oil by the tablespoonful. Fry until golden, 1½ to 2 minutes. Flip the falafels and repeat on the other side. Remove to a paper towel–lined dish. Repeat with the remaining falafel. Keep warm in the oven until ready to serve.

To serve, place a falafel into each lettuce cup. Drizzle with Garlic Tahini Sauce and garnish with a mint leaf.

Garlic Tahini sauce

3 tablespoons tahini (sesame-seed paste)

1 garlic clove, minced

2 tablespoons honey

1 teaspoon soy sauce

1 teaspoon fresh lemon juice

1 tablespoon chopped fresh parsley

1 tablespoon chopped fresh mint

Pinch kosher salt

Put the tahini, garlic, honey, soy sauce, lemon juice, and 2 tablespoons water into a bowl and whisk until smooth. Stir in the chopped herbs and the salt and refrigerate until ready to use. Bring to room temperature before serving. Yield: ¾ cup

Buffet Hors d'oeuvres

We had a very wealthy client with a lakeside home and acres of grounds who was throwing an outdoor afternoon soiree. It was an elegant affair but simple in its execution. It included many of the hors d'oeuvres you'll find in this chapter, all meant to be easily snacked on with fingers or small forks and six-inch plates. When we arrived that day, the weather had become unbelievably perfect; it was the kind of day that keeps Chicagoans from packing it all in during the winter. So perfect, in fact, that our client decided to move the entire event from his back patio (next to the kitchen) down to his dock (next to the lake).

We had no choice but to agree to his request, but I'm telling you, this guy's land was so expansive that the dock was about half a city block from the house. Trying to keep the buffet filled was a nightmare, and the staff became so winded from the trek that service began to suffer. I chastised a waiter over the fact that the Stilton and Pear Tart needed to be replenished.

"Steve," he said, "the problem is that the house is really, really far away. I grabbed the subway from the dock up to the pool house, but I still had to wait to transfer to an express bus that would take me to the kitchen. I didn't have exact change for the bus, so I had to hitchhike around to the dining room and then borrow a bike to get to the pantry."

This taught me two important things: One, make sure your buffet is not too far from where you are keeping the food, and two, I need to stop hiring out-of-work actors.

wine-soaked figs and goat cheese

Yield: 2½ cups
Preparation time: 15 minutes
Cooking time: 20 minutes

10 ounces dried Mission figs

1½ cups dry red wine

1 tablespoon sugar

¼ teaspoon kosher salt

3 sprigs fresh thyme

8 ounces goat cheese

Freshly ground black pepper
to taste

Fresh thyme sprig, for garnish

Good Italian man that he was, my grandfather used to make his own wine. He also had his own fig tree in the backyard. Now if you don't know this, fig trees are supposed to live in warmer climates than Long Island's, but that didn't stop my grandfather from planting them anyway. Every summer the tree would produce fat, juicy figs, deep purple on the outside and a pale pink and white when you broke them open. As the weather turned cold, we would have to wrap the tree in blankets, pink fiberglass insulation, and tar paper to keep it warm. The top always got crowned with an old, battered, upside-down pasta pot. You could always tell the Italian houses in our neighborhood by the tar stick in the front yard. So, Grandpa—this recipe's in memory of you.

Cut the figs in half and put them into a medium-size pot. Add the wine, sugar, salt, and thyme, place the pot over medium heat, and bring the mixture to a boil. Stir once, reduce the heat to low, cover the pot, and let simmer until the figs have soaked up most of the liquid, about 20 minutes. Transfer to a bowl and let cool.

Crumble the goat cheese separately and toss half in with the figs. Put the figs in a decorative bowl and sprinkle with the remaining goat cheese. Hit it with a few grinds of fresh pepper and garnish with a fresh thyme sprig. Serve with a loaf of crusty Italian bread.

ricotta salata with freshly sliced pears and pear balsamic vinegar

Here's one with a lot of wow factor for virtually no work! I've served this to friends before dinner, and they've always been bowled over by the combination of the sweet pear, salty cheese, and tangy complexity of the vinegar drizzle.

Core the pears and cut them into thin slices. Cut the cheese into two wedges and lean the wedges against each other on a decorative platter or slab of marble. Mound the pear slices around the cheese and sprinkle the whole with a little of the balsamic. Pour the remaining balsamic into a decorative bowl for dipping. Garnish the platter with the rosemary sprigs. Serve immediately, as the pears will brown if allowed to sit.

COOK'S NOTE: Ricotta salata is a firm, pure-white cheese with a salty, milky flavor.

pear rosemary balsamic vinegar

1 cup white balsamic vinegar

2 teaspoons sugar

½ ripe pear, roughly chopped

1 sprig rosemary

Place the ingredients in a saucepan over high heat. Bring to a boil, reduce the heat immediately, and let simmer for 15 to 20 minutes. Strain and let cool 30 minutes before serving. Yield: ¾ cup

Yield: 10–12 servings
Preparation time: 10 minutes
Cooking time: 20 minutes

2 ripe pears (red Anjou are my favorite)

1 pound ricotta salata cheese (see note)

½ cup Pear Rosemary Balsamic Vinegar, recipe follows

Rosemary sprigs, for garnish

MAKE AHEAD

Vinegar may be made up to 2 weeks in advance and stored in the refrigerator.

Fresh Mozzarella with Basil and crushed red pepper

Yield: 2 cups
Preparation time: 10 minutes

1 pound fresh mozzarella ciliegine ("little balls")

¼ cup extra-virgin olive oil

½ teaspoon kosher salt

½ teaspoon crushed red pepper

Generous freshly ground black pepper

¼ cup basil chiffonade (see Caprese Cups pg. 31)

My mother will kill me for sharing this, but until I was about eighteen, I had no idea that mozzarella came in any form other than the rubbery and strangely squeaky stuff they sold in our town's supermarket. When I finally tasted fresh mozzarella, the velvety texture and delicate flavor was a revelation to me, and it combines perfectly with equally fresh ingredients to become one of the centerpieces of a beautiful antipasto platter.

Put the mozzarella in a bowl and add the olive oil, salt, and both peppers. Toss well. Add basil and toss again.

Let sit at room temperature for 30 minutes before serving so the flavors can blend. Serve with toothpicks or, if you're like my family, just let people use their fingers!

the well-dressed table

If you've got a handsome table for your buffet, there's just no need to completely cover it. Let the table show through and protect certain areas from crumbs or spillage with pools of cloth. A relaxed, loosely gathered cloth can smartly tie all the aspects of a table together. It's easy to create a unified look by weaving a runner or a contrasting colored cloth into the bread basket, under a few of the different dishes, and off the front of the table. Just remember to make it look comfortable and easy and that centered and symmetrical isn't always good.

Have a favorite cloth that seems unusable due to a stain or tear? Imperfections are easily hidden between folds and under platters. For unique looks, we will often use vintage flea market cloths, Mexican serapes, and other unusual fabrics as foof. That's a professional catering term, by the way. Caterers refer to smaller cloths and runners as "foof." Listen, I'm not proud of it. I'm just relaying information.

vuelve la vida

Vuelve la Vida literally translated means "return to life." I think of it as a cross between gazpacho and ceviche. It's the traditional hangover cure served on beaches in Mexico. I know that from experience—Steve and I took a trip to Mexico a few years back and spent a week lying by the ocean. One night we went to a tequila bar where they served the liquor not with the salt and lime as we know it, but with a tomato juice type of chaser. I thought it was such a great idea that I just kept trying different kinds of tequila. The next morning our concierge, noticing my hangover, suggested a beachside stand which specialized in *Vuelve la Vida*. I made my unsteady way there with a helping hand from Steve, and we got a couple of servings. Not only was it delicious—it worked!

Pour enough olive oil into a large skillet to cover the bottom and place over high heat for 1 minute. Add the squid and sauté with a little salt and pepper until opaque, about 2 minutes. Remove to a large mixing bowl. Add more oil to the pan and repeat the process with the shrimp and scallops, adding them to the mixing bowl when done.

Add the cured catfish to the bowl along with the tomato juice, red onion, cucumber, lime juice and zest, jalapeños, hot sauce, 2 teaspoons salt, cilantro, and green onions. Mix well, cover, and refrigerate for at least 2 hours and up to 1 day so that the flavors can marry. Serve chilled, either in a decorative bowl with tortilla chips on the side or in small coffee cups with teaspoons. Either way, garnish with lime wedges and chopped cilantro.

cured catfish

8 ounces catfish fillet, diced

1 cup fresh lime juice (about 8 limes)

2 teaspoons kosher salt

Put the catfish in a mixing bowl with the lime juice and salt and toss well. Cover and refrigerate at least 8 hours and up to 12 hours.

Yield: 1½ quarts
Preparation time: 50 minutes
Cooking time: 10 minutes

Olive oil

4 ounces squid tubes and tentacles, chopped

Kosher salt and freshly ground black pepper

4 ounces shrimp, peeled and deveined

4 ounces bay scallops

4 ounces canned lump crab meat

Cured Catfish, recipe follows

2 cups tomato juice

¼ cup minced red onion

¼ cup seeded, minced cucumber

Fresh juice and zest of 2 limes (¼ cup juice)

2 jalapeños, seeded and minced

1 teaspoon hot sauce

2 tablespoons chopped cilantro, plus additional for garnish

2 tablespoons chopped green onions

Lime wedges, for garnish

MAKE AHEAD

The Vuelve la Vida can be made the day before.

goat cheese and roasted red pepper torte

Yield: 9-inch tart
Preparation time: 25 minutes
Cooking time: 45 minutes

CORNMEAL PEPPERCORN CRUST

1 cup all-purpose flour

¾ cup cornmeal

2 teaspoons kosher salt

1 teaspoon freshly ground black pepper

¾ cup (1½ sticks) unsalted butter, chilled and cut into bits

3 tablespoons ice water

FILLING

6 tablespoons butter, softened

7 ounces goat cheese, softened

2 eggs

½ cup sour cream

¼ cup chopped fresh basil

2 roasted red peppers, cut into strips

SPECIAL EQUIPMENT

9-inch disposable foil cake pan

Pie weights (or dry rice or beans)

MAKE AHEAD

The torte can be made and refrigerated up to 3 days in advance.

This is a versatile recipe. It pairs beautifully with a simple green salad on a brunch buffet, as well as standing on its own on an hors d'oeuvre buffet. We made a whole slew of them for various New Year's Eve parties one year and had a couple left over. The next day, on our way to a New Year's Day brunch, I stopped by the catering kitchen and picked one up. We brought it to the brunch, and as it turned out, it went so quickly that I wound up going back to get the other one.

Preheat the oven to 350 degrees F.

To make the crust, place the flour, cornmeal, salt, and pepper in the bowl of a food processor. Add the butter and pulse until the mixture resembles little peas. Place the mixture in a bowl and add the water 1 tablespoon at a time, stirring with a fork to incorporate. Do not overwork.

Press the dough into the tart pan, making sure to work it up the sides of the pan. Place in the freezer for 10 minutes. Remove the crust from the freezer, line it with foil, and fill with the pie weights (or rice or beans). Bake for 10 minutes, then remove the foil and bake another 5 minutes. Remove from oven and set aside.

For the filling, put the butter and goat cheese into the bowl of a mixer and beat until well incorporated, 2 to 3 minutes. Beat in the eggs 1 at a time, then add the sour cream. Mix well. Chop half the red pepper strips to make ¼ cup. Fold in the basil and chopped red peppers. Pour the mix into the prepared shell and arrange the remaining pepper slices on the top like the spokes of a wheel. Place in the oven for 25 to 30 minutes, or until the filling is set and the top is lightly brown. Let cool completely before chilling for a minimum of 1 hour. This will set the custard and make it easier to slice. You can cut or tear the disposable pan from the torte. Place on a decorative plate and bring back to room temperature before serving.

three-mushroom tart

OK, I'm going to 'fess up here and now about my handling of mushrooms. It's commonly noted that you shouldn't wash them. But if I'm going to cook them right away, I find it's faster and easier to rinse off the dirt. It won't compromise the taste or texture at all. There, I've said it. Go ahead and call the food police.

Prepare and partially bake the crust.

Preheat the oven to 350 degrees F.

Place the shiitakes into a medium-size saucepan and cover with cold water. Place the saucepan over a medium flame and bring to a boil. Reduce the heat and simmer for 15 minutes. This will reconstitute the mushrooms. Once they've softened, let them cool. Remove the stems and slice them to ¼-inch thickness. Set aside.

In a large sauté pan, melt the butter over medium heat, making sure not to let it brown. Add the onion and cook until translucent, about 10 minutes.

Add the fresh mushrooms to the pan. Add the basil, dried and fresh thyme, salt, and pepper. Stir well and let cook for 15 minutes, or until most of the liquid has evaporated. Add the shiitakes, red wine, and tomato paste and simmer until thickened.

Spoon into the prepared crust and bake for 20 minutes. Remove the tart from the oven and let cool to room temperature. Remove the ring and slide the tart onto a decorative plate. Slightly lift one side of the tart and peel back the parchment. Ease the tart back down and continue to gently pull the parchment until it slides out from under the tart. Slice into wedges, garnish with the fresh thyme, and serve.

Yield: 10-inch tart
Preparation time: 30 minutes
Cooking time: 20 minutes

1 recipe Cornmeal Peppercorn Crust, see page 52

2 ounces dried shiitakes

3 ounces portobellos, trimmed and sliced

½ pound white mushrooms, trimmed and sliced

6 tablespoons unsalted butter

1 small yellow onion, thinly sliced

½ teaspoon dried basil

½ teaspoon dried thyme

4 sprigs fresh thyme, plus additional for garnish

Kosher salt and freshly ground pepper to taste

1 tablespoon tomato paste

⅓ cup dry red wine

SPECIAL EQUIPMENT

10-inch springform pan

10-inch parchment circle

Pie weights (or dry rice or beans)

MAKE AHEAD

The tart can be made 2 days in advance and refrigerated. Bring to room temperature before serving.

stilton and pear tart

Pictured on page 203

Yield: 20–24 pieces
Preparation time: 30 minutes
Cooking time: 55 minutes

CRUST

1 ¼ cups all-purpose flour,
plus additional for rolling

½ teaspoon kosher salt

1 teaspoon freshly ground
black pepper

7 tablespoons unsalted
butter chilled

3 tablespoons ice water

FILLING

½ cup sour cream

2 large eggs

6 tablespoons unsalted butter,
melted

10 ounces crumbled Stilton

1 teaspoon kosher salt

½ teaspoon freshly ground
black pepper

1 pear, peeled, cored and
thinly sliced

6 fresh sage leaves

SPECIAL EQUIPMENT

10-inch tart pan with
removable bottom

Pie weights (or dry rice or
beans)

Steve's mom is from England and loves a good wedge of Stilton. Trying to score brownie points during one of her visits, I put together this tart and served it at a party we threw in her honor. She loved it, and I am now forever in her good graces!

Preheat oven to 350 degrees F.

To make the crust, put the flour, salt, and pepper into the bowl of a food processor fitted with a steel blade. Cut the butter into bits and add to the flour. Pulse until the mixture resembles small peas. Transfer to a mixing bowl and, using a fork to mix, add the ice water 1 tablespoon at a time. Once the dough has formed a ball, flatten into a disk, wrap in plastic wrap, and refrigerate for 1 hour.

Remove the dough from the refrigerator, place it on a floured surface, and roll out to a 12-inch diameter. Place in the tart pan, pushing the dough gently into the edges and forming it to the crimped sides. Using a fork, prick the flat surface of the dough all over. Refrigerate for 15 minutes.

Cover the tart shell with foil and weigh down with pie weights (raw rice or beans work well). Place it in the bottom half of the oven for 15 minutes. Remove foil and bake 10 more minutes. Remove from oven and set aside.

To make the filling, put the sour cream in a large mixing bowl. Whisk in the eggs. Next whisk in the melted butter. Fold in the Stilton, salt, and pepper using a rubber spatula. Pour the mixture into the prebaked crust, smoothing the top with the spatula. Arrange the sliced pears to look like the spokes of a wheel, alternating with the sage leaves.

Place the tart in the top half of the oven and bake for 30 minutes, or until the top of the tart starts to turn a golden brown. Remove and let cool. Remove the side ring of the pan, cover with plastic wrap, and refrigerate until ready to serve. Slice into wedges and serve. Can also be made as individual tarts.

MAKE AHEAD: The tart can be made the day before.

spinach, artichoke, and bacon dip

Spinach dip is an American classic, and everyone needs a good recipe for it. Here's mine—with the green taste of spinach, the tanginess of the marinated artichoke hearts, and the salty smokiness of bacon. To impress guests even further, buy an unsliced loaf of Pullman bread. Starting about an inch from the side of the loaf, hollow it out by cutting out a large rectangle—just make sure not to cut through the bottom. Scoop out the inside and fill it with the dip. It makes a phenomenal presentation.

Heat the vegetable oil in a small skillet over medium-low heat. Add the garlic and shallot and cook, stirring frequently, until the shallot softens and the garlic begins to brown, about 7 minutes. Remove from heat and set aside.

Put the spinach in a colander and squeeze all the excess water out of it. Transfer it to a large mixing bowl and add the artichoke hearts, bacon, cooked garlic and shallot, lemon zest, sour cream, salt, and pepper. Mix well with a rubber spatula and transfer to a decorative bowl. Allow to sit for 30 minutes before serving so the flavors can marry. Serve with Savory Pita Crisps.

Yield: 4 cups
Preparation Time: 20 minutes
Cooking Time: 15 minutes

1 tablespoon vegetable oil

3 cloves garlic, minced

1 shallot, minced

10-ounce package frozen chopped spinach, thawed

6-ounce jar marinated artichoke hearts, roughly chopped

10 bacon strips, fried until crisp and crumbled

1 teaspoon lemon zest

2 cups sour cream

1 teaspoon kosher salt

1 teaspoon freshly ground black pepper

Savory Pita Crisps (see page 66)

tarts and all

Here are two pointers for avoiding tart and piecrust disaster. The first is to refrigerate your cooked tart and slice it cold. You'll get a nice clean cut, and you can let it come up to room temperature before serving. Another is to use a pan with a removable bottom, and simply leave the tart on the tart pan base. Fill a larger platter with leafy greens like mint or lemon leaves and place your tart, including the base, right on top for a beautiful presentation. Of course, if you've read this tip too late, you can always grab some fresh herbs or berries and artistically hide your gaffe. Not that I'm speaking from experience . . .

MAKE AHEAD

The dip can be made the day before.

rosemary gorgonzola mushrooms in boule

Yield: 2½ cups
Preparation time: 15 minutes
Cooking time: 30 minutes

½ **pound white mushrooms**

½ **pound baby portobello mushrooms**

4 **tablespoons (½ stick) unsalted butter**

2 **tablespoons olive oil**

½ **Spanish onion, thinly sliced**

4 **sprigs fresh rosemary**

¼ **cup dry white wine**

4 **ounces Gorgonzola**

1 **cup heavy cream**

1 **teaspoon kosher salt**

Generous freshly ground pepper

12-**inch sourdough boule, top sliced off and soft inner bread pulled out.**

1 **baguette, sliced**

MAKE AHEAD

The mushrooms can be cooked with the wine (before the cheese and cream are added) the day before. Reheat the mixture to continue.

Here's another "wow factor" recipe. It's delicious, can be made ahead of time, and makes a great presentation on a buffet. What more can you ask?

Rinse the mushrooms well, cut off and discard the ends of the stems, and slice them about ¼ inch thick. Set aside.

Put the butter and olive oil into a large skillet and set over medium heat.

Add the onion to the pan. Reduce the heat to low and cook the onions for 15 minutes until translucent. Add the mushrooms and rosemary, raise the heat to medium, and cook, stirring occasionally, until the mushrooms give up their liquid. Let the mixture simmer until the mushroom liquid has reduced by three quarters. Add the white wine and reduce again until the pan is almost dry.

Add the Gorgonzola and cream. Bring to a simmer and reduce by half, stirring occasionally. Stir in the salt and pepper and spoon into the hollowed-out boule. Mound sliced baguettes around the boule and serve immediately.

water, water everywhere

Pouring water is a simple task. However, most of us make a mess of it after we've set a beautiful table. One of the things that we do when catering weddings is to fill our glasses with ice before the guests arrive. About 10 minutes before dinner service, we top the glasses with water using a pitcher that has no ice. You'll get a much smoother and neater pour without the cubes of ice alternately blocking and speeding the water's flow. The second tip is to always bring the glass to the pitcher rather than vice versa. By picking up the glass and holding it away from the table you eliminate the possibility of spills and drips across your tablecloth. I know, it's so easy, makes so much sense . . . so why did it take me so long to figure it out?

And you know what else we love? It's nothing groundbreaking, but a thin slice of lemon in the water glass is still the simplest and least expensive way of making an elegant impression.

Gorgonzola, Fig, and Pecan cheese Terrine

Cheese terrines are another signature of The Hearty Boys. Every party we cater has at least two of our terrines sent to it. This particular recipe was created for our audition tape for *The Next Food Network Star*. We shot it in our catering test kitchen using our office Christmas tree for extra lighting. I'm still amazed they were able to see us well enough to choose us.

Put ½ cup of the figs into a small saucepan along with the red wine and the thyme. Let the mixture simmer over low heat for 15 minutes. Drain the figs, discard the thyme and wine, and set the figs aside to cool.

Put the cream cheese and butter into the bowl of an electric stand mixer and, using the paddle attachment, cream the mixture on medium until well blended, about 1 minute. Add the Gorgonzola, brandy, and salt and beat 1 more minute. Do not overbeat the terrine or it won't set properly.

Spray the loaf pan with cooking spray and line the inside with plastic wrap. Spoon half of the cheese mixture into the pan and spread it evenly, making sure to get into the corners. Scatter the cooked figs, ½ cup of the pecans, and the parsley on top evenly and cover with the remaining cheese. Give the pan a few sharp raps on a flat surface to settle the terrine, cover it with plastic wrap, and refrigerate for at least 6 hours.

To remove the terrine from the pan, turn the pan upside down on a flat surface and pull one end of the plastic wrap down. The terrine will slip out of the pan onto the top piece of plastic wrap. Slice the terrine and fan out the pieces on a platter garnished with greens. Garnish with the remaining figs, pecans, and parsley. Serve with water crackers or other good quality crackers.

Yield: About 16 servings
Preparation Time: 30 minutes

1 cup quartered dried
Mission figs

1 cup dry red wine

1 sprig fresh thyme

1 pound cream cheese,
at room temperature

1½ sticks unsalted butter, at
room temperature

8 ounces Gorgonzola, crumbled

2 tablespoons brandy

1 teaspoon kosher salt

1 cup pecans, toasted

2 tablespoons chopped
flat-leaf parsley, plus additional
leaves for garnish

SPECIAL EQUIPMENT

9-by-5-inch loaf pan

Cooking spray and plastic wrap

MAKE AHEAD

The terrine can be made up to
1 week in advance.

pissaladière

Yield: 64 pieces
Preparation time: 15 minutes
Cooking time: 1 hour

2 tablespoons extra-virgin olive oil

2 Spanish onions, thinly-sliced

3 cloves garlic, minced

1 tablespoon anchovy paste

1 sprig fresh thyme, plus additional sprigs for garnish

1 sprig fresh rosemary

1 teaspoon dried lavender (optional)

⅓ cup sun-dried tomatoes, rehydrated and sliced into thin strips

12-inch square puff pastry sheet, thawed

¼ cup sliced pitted kalamata olives, sliced

MAKE AHEAD

The onion mixture can be made the day before. The tart should be baked day of.

Right after I graduated from college, I bought a backpack and went to Europe for a month. I did all the starving-student things you do in Europe—bought a cheap rail pass, stayed in youth hostels or on the beach, drank a lot of strong coffee, and ate a lot of bread and pastries. The whole time on the trains, fellow travelers kept telling me that when I got to Nice I had to try the pizza. I figured I'd give it a shot (although, being an Italian from New York, I was a little skeptical).

When I arrived in that beautiful city on the Riviera, one of the first things I did was find a café that was serving these small, thin-crusted pizzas. They were loaded with onions that were sweet yet salty. When I was able to find a waiter I could communicate with, I asked him what exactly I was eating. He told me it was a pissaladière—named for the *pissala*, or anchovy paste, that the onions were cooked with. It was delicious, and when I got back home, I tried to re-create the flavors. It's evolved over the years into this present form. I hope you enjoy it as much as I did all those years ago in Nice.

Preheat the oven to 350 degrees F.

Pour the olive oil into a large skillet and place over medium heat for 2 minutes. Add the onions and garlic and cook, stirring often, until the onions turn translucent. Add the anchovy paste and herbs, reduce the heat to low, and cook, stirring occasionally, until the mixture caramelizes and turns a golden brown, about 30 minutes.

Remove the skillet from the heat and stir in the tomatoes.

Gently unfold the puff pastry sheet and lay it flat on a baking sheet. Using a fork, prick the pastry all over. Spread the onion mixture evenly onto the pastry, leaving a ½-inch border on all sides. Sprinkle with the olives and place in the bottom half of the oven for 20 to 30 minutes, or until the pastry bottom is golden.

Remove the tart from the oven and let cool about 30 minutes before slicing into 1½-inch squares. Garnish with fresh thyme and serve at room temperature.

smoked salmon, vodka, and caviar dip

Pictured on page 45

Yield: 2 cups
Preparation time: 15 minutes

What a lot of people don't know is that I'm a bit of a Russophile. I love to read about Imperial Russia, and that was the inspiration for this recipe. Caviar and vodka are quintessentially Russian, so I thought, Why not create a dip using them? Here it is—and, may I say, *na zdorovje!*

Put the smoked salmon, sour cream, vodka, lemon juice, onion, dill, salt, pepper, and heaping tablespoon of the caviar into a large bowl and, using a rubber spatula, fold until well mixed.

Transfer the dip to a decorative bowl and mound the 2 teaspoons caviar in the center. Garnish with fresh dill sprigs and serve with crackers or Savory Pita Crisps.

½ **pound smoked salmon, finely chopped**

½ **cup sour cream**

1 **tablespoon vodka**

2 **tablespoons fresh lemon juice**

2 **tablespoons minced red onion**

1 **teaspoon chopped fresh dill, plus fresh dill sprigs for garnish**

¼ **teaspoon kosher salt**

½ **teaspoon freshly ground black pepper**

1 **heaping tablespoon plus 2 teaspoons red lumpfish caviar, rinsed**

Savory Pita Crisps (see page 66)

chilly receptions

We had a client who had just moved into a terrific high-rise with spectacular views of downtown Chicago and the lake. His apartment was more or less a studio, so he had planned a rooftop deck event. We ordered tall cocktail tables for leaning, did all the linens in classic cocktail-party black, and covered the bar and the railings in tiny sparkling votive candles. The city was a spectacular backdrop for an elegant evening affair.

Unfortunately, he neglected to tell any of his guests that this was an outdoor event, so all these unsuspecting women turned up in little black dresses and stood twenty floors above the city, huddled and shivering against the walls of the building. We had to move the entire party (food, guests, tables, bar, everything) down into his one-room studio apartment. Within the hour, most of his guests left.

So, outdoor parties are a great idea, but warn your guests of the location so they can dress appropriately. And if you've ever seen a woman caught Prada-heel deep in soft grass, you'll understand why this rule applies to lawn parties too.

MAKE AHEAD

The dip can be made up to 2 days in advance.

blue cheese and caramelized onion dip

Yield: 2 cups
Preparation time: 10 minutes
Cooking time: 20 minutes

1 tablespoon vegetable oil

1 large onion, thinly sliced

¾ cup good quality mayonnaise, such as Hellmann's

¾ cup sour cream

4 ounces crumbly blue cheese, room temperature

Kosher salt and freshly ground black pepper to taste

When I was a kid, my parents would let my friends and me pitch a tent in the backyard on summer nights and camp out. We'd spend most of the nights stuffing ourselves with junk food and seeing who could tell the scariest stories. One of our favorite snacks was potato chips with onion dip. My mom would whip up the old standard—sour cream and onion soup mix.

My mouth still waters for onion dip, so I came up with this grown-up version. It's reminiscent of childhood, but it's also a little more sophisticated, with the sweetness of the caramelized onions and the sharpness of the blue cheese.

Heat the oil in a heavy medium-size saucepan over medium-low heat. Add the onions and cook, stirring occasionally, until the onions are deep golden brown, about 20 minutes. Let cool.

Whisk together mayonnaise and sour cream in medium-size bowl. Add the blue cheese and, using rubber spatula, mash the mixture until it is smooth. Stir in the caramelized onions. Season the dip with salt and pepper.

Cover and refrigerate until flavors blend, at least 2 hours. Serve dip chilled or at room temperature.

talking trash

Did you ever get caught holding a used coffee stirrer or beverage napkin for what seemed like the entire length of a get-together? And you don't want to leave trash on an end table or near the buffet food, so you hide it in your shirt pocket and find it again when you're changing for bed? Or is that just me? At casual gatherings, make it easier for your guests to drop off small trash items by placing a little basket on your buffet. Just remember to preplace one coffee stirrer or used sugar packet in the basket so guests know why it's there. Be sure to empty it frequently during your party, and I guarantee you'll find fewer bevnaps hiding in your ficus later that day. Oh, come on, now—you know you've done that!

MAKE AHEAD

The dip can be made up to 2 days in advance

rosemary-scented Hummus

I'm still always surprised when I see people at the market with prepared hummus in their baskets. It's quick and inexpensive to make at home, and you can tailor it to your own tastes. Try adding some crushed red pepper for a spicier hummus or half a roasted red pepper for a smoky sweet taste. Go ahead—experiment and make this recipe your own.

Put the chickpeas, tahini, garlic, lemon juice, lemon zest, and rosemary in the bowl of a food processor and process until smooth. Add some of the reserved liquid if the hummus is too thick; it should be creamy. Finish by stirring in the olive oil, salt, and pepper. Serve with Savory Pita Crisps.

height and interest

There is one phrase that I rely upon in setting up a buffet, and that phrase is "height and interest." When I use it (and I frequently do), my staff snicker at me. I know they think I sound like a catering freak, but I'd just like to point out that I'm writing a book, and they are not.

As far as height is concerned, every buffet needs a focal point. Something tall—not necessarily centered and not necessarily floral. You can use anything from a flea market pedestal topped with cheeses and fruits to a very tall glass vase filled with lemons. And be sure to vary the heights of everything on the table. I mean everything. When setting out stacks of buffet plates, do three stacks at different heights.

For interest, do the visually unexpected with your food. For dips, experiment with terra-cotta flowerpots (plug the holes with plastic wrap), colorful oversized café au lait mugs, or shallow vintage vases. Put a charcuterie on an antique pizza paddle or Amaretto Profiteroles and chocolate-covered strawberries on a broken slab of marble.

Food lined up all straight and regimented looks unappealing. Just keep repeating "height and interest" and ignore the snickering masses.

Yield: 2½ cups
Preparation time: 10 minutes

2 cups canned chickpeas, drained and liquid reserved

⅔ cup tahini (sesame-seed paste)

2–3 cloves garlic, minced

⅔ cup fresh lemon juice

Zest of 1 lemon

1 tablespoon finely chopped fresh rosemary

2 tablespoons extra-virgin olive oil

2 teaspoons kosher salt

Freshly ground black pepper to taste

Savory Pita Crisps (see page 66)

MAKE AHEAD

The hummus can be made up to 4 days in advance.

mushroom hazelnut pâté

This savory vegetarian pâté suits even a meat lover's palate! The meatiness of the mushrooms pairs beautifully with the creaminess of the custard, and the crunchiness of the hazelnuts is a nice surprise. Our executive catering chef, Jericho, is a vegetarian, and he swears by this pâté. He'll often take leftovers home and make a meal out of it. You can't get a better recommendation than that!

Preheat oven to 350 degrees F.

Spray the loaf pan with the cooking spray and line it with parchment paper, making sure to cover the bottom and two longer sides of the pan.

Melt the butter in a large skillet over medium heat. Add the onion and garlic and cook 15 to 20 minutes, or until translucent. Add the mushrooms and cook 30 minutes, or until mixture begins to stick together a bit.

Meanwhile, in a separate bowl, beat the eggs and cream together. Mix in a ½ cup of the hazelnuts and the thyme, chopped parsley, bread crumbs, lemon juice, salt, and pepper. Add mushroom mix and stir to combine well. Pour into the prepared loaf pan, cover with foil, and set in a larger pan. Fill the outer pan halfway with water and place in the preheated oven. Bake until center is set, about 1 hour. Remove from oven and let cool before refrigerating for at least 6 hours.

When it's time for the party, remove the pâté from the refrigerator, run a sharp knife around the sides of the pan and, using the sides of the parchment, lift the pâté out. Remove the parchment and slice. Arrange the pâté slices on a platter and garnish with fresh parsley leaves and the remaining ½ cup of hazelnuts.

MAKE AHEAD: The pâté can be made up to 3 days in advance.

Yield: About 16 servings
Preparation time: 1 hour
Cooking time: 1 hour

½ cup (1 stick) unsalted butter

1 onion, minced

2 cloves garlic, minced

1½ pounds white mushrooms, trimmed and sliced

4 eggs

1 cup heavy cream

1 cup coarsely chopped toasted hazelnuts

2 teaspoons dried thyme

¼ cup chopped fresh parsley, plus the remainder of the bunch, left whole, for garnish

½ cup dried bread crumbs

1½ tablespoons fresh lemon juice

2 teaspoons kosher salt

1 teaspoon freshly ground black pepper

SPECIAL EQUIPMENT

9-by-5-inch loaf pan

Cooking spray and parchment

Large, deep baking pan

savory pita crisps

Yield: 48 pita crisps
Preparation Time: 10 minutes
Cooking Time: 20 minutes

1½ teaspoons kosher salt

1½ teaspoons dried basil

1 teaspoon garlic powder

1 teaspoon onion powder

½ teaspoon dried oregano

½ teaspoon freshly ground
black pepper

¼ teaspoon celery salt

4 sandwich-sized pita breads,
cut into 12 wedges each

¼ cup vegetable oil

MAKE AHEAD

The crisps can be made up to
1 week in advance and stored
in an airtight container.

Don't you hate people who double dip? I mean where did that behavior come from? We catered a party at one of Chicago's museums when we first opened The Hearty Boys and about halfway through the evening I noticed this guy hovering over the dips—not double dipping but triple dipping! Luckily no one else was nearby and when he moved on I quickly replaced the dips. From that point on I started cutting the pita wedges smaller before toasting them. Less surface area equals less double dipping.

Preheat the oven to 350 degrees F.

Mix all the herbs and spices in a small bowl. Put the pita wedges into a large mixing bowl and add the spice mix. Drizzle the oil over all and toss well to coat. Put the pitas onto a baking sheet, shake it to even them out and place the pan in the top half of the oven.

Bake the pitas until they are crispy and lightly brown, about 20 minutes. Remove from the oven, let cool 10 minutes, and mound around the dip bowl.

peppered rosemary oat crackers

This is a fun little recipe for an interesting cracker. It stands on its own, pairs well with cheese, or makes a savory base for passed hors d'oeuvres.

Preheat oven to 375 degrees F.

Put the oats into a food processor and pulse until finely chopped. Add the flour, salt, pepper, rosemary, baking powder, and butter and pulse until mixture resembles coarse meal. Add the milk and pulse until a dough forms, about 15 seconds.

On a lightly floured surface, roll the dough out ⅛-inch thick (try for a rectangular shape as there will be less waste.) and cut out about 60 square oatcakes. Arrange the oatcakes on baking sheets 1 inch apart and bake in middle of the oven for 12 to 15 minutes, or until lightly brown on the bottom. Transfer oatcakes to a rack and cool completely.

take your supplements

If you're having more than 50 guests, take off a bit of pressure by ordering some supplemental foods! Most supermarkets carry bean dips and similar prepared foods that are easily dressed up by mixing in fresh herbs. Your guests will never know your dirty little store-bought secret. The bulk warehouse stores offer tasty imports like canned or jarred dolmades (rolled grape leaves), mini frozen quiches and bite-sized fruit tartlets. Make these your own by drizzling the dolmades in extra-virgin olive oil before rolling them in freshly cut mint; add a quarter slice of Gruyère to the quiches before reheating them; and dust the tartlets with powdered confectioners' sugar. We've even taken advantage of frozen pigs in a blanket by serving them alongside a homemade wasabi lime mustard for an upscale kick. Take help where you can get it, because if you don't purchase some items, you will end up having to prepare hundreds of little things.

Yield: 50–60 pieces
Preparation time: 20 minutes
Cooking time: 12–15 minutes

2 cups old-fashioned rolled oats

¼ cup plus 2 tablespoons all-purpose flour, plus additional for rolling

2 teaspoons kosher salt

1 teaspoon freshly ground black pepper

½ teaspoon chopped rosemary

¾ teaspoon baking powder

4 tablespoons (½ stick) cold unsalted butter, cut into bits

¼ cup plus 2 tablespoons whole milk

MAKE AHEAD

The crackers can be made up to 1 week in advance and stored in an airtight container.

basic crostini with variations

Yield: 30
Preparation Time: 10 minutes
Cooking Time: 15 minutes

1 baguette, sliced in ½-inch pieces (about 30)

4 tablespoons (½ stick) unsalted butter, melted

2 tablespoons olive oil

Kosher salt and freshly ground black pepper

SPECIAL EQUIPMENT

Pastry brush

Crostini form the base for a lot of passed hors d'oeuvres. We use them, along with other bread and cracker bases, to make a myriad of canapés. They can be flavored in any number of ways, but here's a tip. Keep a close eye on them when they're in the oven. I can tell you from experience they burn easily.

Preheat the oven to 350 degrees F.

Lay the baguette slices out on a sheet pan. Mix the butter and olive oil together and brush the mix liberally onto each slice. Sprinkle with salt and pepper. Place the pan in the top half of the oven and bake until slightly golden, about 15 minutes.

garlic parmesan crostini

Add to basic recipe: **2 cloves garlic, minced**
                         ½ cup shredded Parmesan

Put the butter, olive oil, and garlic into a saucepan and place over medium heat. Let the mixture simmer for 5 minutes to infuse with the garlic flavor. Proceed as above. Sprinkle liberally with the Parmesan before adding the salt and pepper.

herbed crostini

Add to basic recipe: **1 tablespoon finely chopped fresh parsley**
                         1 teaspoon finely chopped fresh rosemary
                         1 teaspoons dried basil
                         ½ teaspoon dried thyme
                         ½ teaspoon dried ground sage

Put the butter, olive oil, parsley, rosemary, basil, thyme, and sage into a saucepan and place over medium heat. Let simmer for 5 minutes. Proceed as above, taking care to brush some of the herbs onto each crostini.

MAKE AHEAD

The crostini can be made up to 1 week in advance and stored in an airtight container.

spiced cocktail nuts

Our friend Loretta has a signature recipe that she makes and brings to parties instead of a bottle of wine. I've tried as hard as I can to drag it out of her, but she's not giving it up. So I put together my own recipe, which I'm going to start bringing to the same parties. It's going to be dueling cocktail nuts, Loretta!

Preheat the oven to 350 degrees F.

Put the nuts in a mixing bowl and set aside.

Put the butter into a small saucepan and place over medium heat. As the butter melts, add the thyme, rosemary, cumin, sugar, mustard, cayenne, allspice, and pepper. Allow to simmer for 1 minute. Pour the butter mixture over the nuts, add the salt, and toss well to coat.

Spread the nuts on a baking sheet in one layer, then bake until the nuts are a golden brown, about 20 minutes. Remove and let cool before serving.

a cheesy tip

Cheese is the basic building block of every party, and you must always supplement your cocktail parties with a selection. Choose cheese that suits your budget, but always get wonderful artisanal cheeses when you can afford to. Here are a few points for a beautiful presentation:

- Cut a chunk out of your cheeses and leave the knife handy so your guests don't feel funny about making the first cut.
- Take larger rectangular or square blocks of cheese and cut them at angles. Then create visual interest by piling them atop each other.
- Let your crackers and breads spill across the tablecloth. A basket of tightly packed crackers looks a little sad.
- Fill the gaps. Piles of spilling grapes, color-drenched dried fruits, a pomegranate broken in half . . . all these touches make a cheese platter a centerpiece.

Yield: 3 cups
Preparation time: 5 minutes
Cooking time: 20 minutes

3 cups mixed pecans, walnuts, and almonds

2 tablespoons unsalted butter

2 teaspoons chopped fresh thyme leaves

2 rosemary sprigs, needles stripped and finely chopped

1 teaspoon ground cumin

1 teaspoon sugar

½ teaspoon ground mustard

¼ teaspoon cayenne

¼ teaspoon allspice

½ teaspoon white pepper

1 teaspoon kosher salt

MAKE AHEAD

The nuts can be made up to 1 week in advance and stored in an airtight container.

starters

We love to begin with an unusual starter course at large events. People expect to be served a green salad so it's always a treat to surprise them with a creamy plate of Smoked Oyster Polenta or a sweet and savory Herb Braised Pear. We'll often have a soup plate preset on a charger and have the waiters pour steaming hot cream soups from silver jugs. The waiters do this, not me because of the shaking. I've got a hand tremor. It runs in my family—it's no big deal. It's a benign neurological thing that simply makes my hands shake and can be the bane of my existence.

In New York, I used to cater really large parties at the Metropolitan Opera and the Museum of Natural History. The preferred service at these events was Russian plattered (known in America as French service). That's when the waiter has all four courses on one really large, really heavy platter and serves guests with a spoon and fork in one hand while balancing this really large, really heavy platter in the other. Since I'd be behind the guests, they would see only my shaking hand passing across their lap with some sort of juicy beef. They would usually come up with a clever and polite crack like, "Say, why're you so nervous? Don't spill, now!" and make a big gag out of pulling their napkins up to their chins. At that point I'd feel uncomfortable and self-conscious about my God-given affliction—thanks to them for pointing it out in front of the entire table—and my nerves would kick in, causing my hands to vibrate like a rotary sander.

I won't even go into the time at the Iranian embassy when I had to Russian serve a deep red soup to Barbara Walters, Peter Jennings, and Bernard Shaw. I will tell you, however, that every time I saw those damn platters, I would beg and plead to be the guy with the wine bottle. When pouring wine, I was at least able to make it appear as if the shaking was an intricate wine-steward sort of twisting flourish.

It all worked out in the end, though, when we got a new headwaiter who truly understood how difficult my tremor situation was. He confided that every time he got nervous, he'd get a nosebleed and pass out.

Leek and Cremini Ravioli with Red and Yellow Tomato Concassé

Yield: 8 servings
Preparation time: 45 minutes
Cooking time: 20 minutes

¼ cup extra-virgin olive oil

1 large clove garlic, minced

1 bunch leeks, trimmed
and sliced

4 medium-sized cremini
mushrooms, rinsed and
finely diced

4 ounces creamy goat cheese

1 teaspoon kosher salt

½ teaspoon freshly ground
black pepper

32 wonton wrappers
(3-inch squares)

Red and Yellow Tomato
Concassé, recipe follows

Sautéed Swiss Chard,
recipe follows

8 fresh oregano sprigs,
for garnish

Many people shy away from making their own ravioli because it's so labor-intensive, what with making your own pasta from scratch. . . . This recipe cuts that step out by using wonton wrappers. They're easy to work with, and they're also incredibly light, which is perfect for a spring vegetable preparation such as this. Once you've tried this recipe, don't be afraid to change up the filling—there are a million combinations you could try.

In a large skillet and over medium heat, warm the olive oil. Add the garlic and cook until nicely golden brown, about 3 minutes. Add the leeks and cremini, raise the heat to high, and cook, stirring often, until the leeks are wilted and any excess water has evaporated. Remove from heat transfer to a large mixing bowl. Add the goat cheese and salt and pepper and stir to incorporate the goat cheese. Set aside to cool.

When the mixture is cool, lay out all 32 wonton squares on a flat work space. Place about a tablespoon of veggie mixture in the center of 16 of the wonton wrappers. Working in small batches, brush the edges of all the wrappers with water and place the unfilled wrappers on top of the filled ones. Press the edges well to seal and set aside to dry a little.

When all the ravioli are prepared, bring a large pot of salted water to a boil, lower to a gentle simmer and cook the ravioli in two batches. They'll only need 4 or 5 minutes in the water. Be very gentle with them, removing them with a slotted spoon and placing them in a large pan of hot tap water.

To assemble the dish, place a bed of sautéed chard on each plate. Top with two ravioli and pour the warm concassé over all. Garnish with a sprig of fresh oregano.

Pictured on page 71

red and yellow tomato concassé

¼ cup extra-virgin olive oil

2 cloves garlic, minced

2 cups red Roma tomatoes, finely chopped (2–3 tomatoes)

2 cups yellow Roma tomatoes, finely chopped (2–3 tomatoes)

1 sprig fresh oregano

Kosher salt and freshly ground black pepper to taste

Pour the olive oil into a large skillet and place over high heat. Add the garlic and cook until nicely golden, about 3 minutes. Add the chopped tomatoes and oregano sprig, lower the heat, and let cook, covered, until the tomatoes have broken down, 10 to 15 minutes. Remove the oregano sprig before serving. Serve warm. Yield: 2½ cups

sautéed swiss chard

1 tablespoon extra-virgin olive oil

2 bunches rainbow Swiss chard, washed and coarsely chopped, including stems

Juice of ½ lemon

Kosher salt and freshly ground black pepper to taste

Pour the olive oil into a large skillet and place over high heat for 1 minute. Add the chard and, stirring constantly, let it wilt, 2 to 3 minutes. Add the lemon juice, salt, and pepper and cook for 1 more minute. Remove from heat and serve immediately. Yield: 2 cups

MAKE AHEAD

Ravioli can be made up to 5 days in advance and frozen. To cook from frozen, add an additional 1–2 minutes to the cooking time.

Concassé can be made the day before and reheated.

Swiss chard must be made just before serving.

smoked oyster polenta

Yield: 8–10 servings
Preparation time: 20 minutes
Cooking time: 45 minutes

½ pound sliced bacon, cut into
½-inch dice

2 cups coarse polenta

1 tablespoon kosher salt

1 teaspoon white pepper

1 cup fresh baby spinach,
coarsely chopped,
plus additional whole
leaves for garnish

½ cup (1 stick) unsalted butter

Two 4-ounce cans smoked
oysters

Roasted Romas, recipe follows

MAKE AHEAD

Tomatoes can be made the day
before, refrigerated, and reheated
before serving.

A few years ago we were in Hawaii on the beautiful island of Kauai. A group of us went to dinner one night at Roy's. I chose an escargot cassoulet as a starter—creamy polenta topped with snails and oven-roasted tomatoes—it was heaven on a plate. It inspired me to create this dish, my homage to the restaurant's founder and chef, Roy Yamaguchi. The blend of textures and flavors are making my stomach growl as I sit here!

Cook the bacon in a large skillet over high heat, stirring often, until it is very crispy, about 10 minutes. Spoon the bacon onto a paper towel–lined dish to drain. Set aside.

Pour 2 quarts water into a large pot and bring it to a boil over high heat. Add the salt and pepper and slowly begin to sprinkle in the polenta, whisking constantly.

Once all the polenta has been added to the water, exchange the whisk for a wooden spoon, lower the heat to medium, add the chopped spinach, and keep stirring. Cook for 20 minutes, then add the butter and smoked oysters. Stir until the butter has melted and the oysters are well mixed into the polenta.

Serve immediately by laying a few leaves of baby spinach on each plate. Lay one roasted tomato half on the spinach and top this with ½ cup polenta, making sure that the spinach and tomato are peeking out. Sprinkle with the reserved bacon and serve.

roasted Romas

4 or 5 Roma tomatoes, cut in half   ½ teaspoon kosher salt

½ cup olive oil   ¼ teaspoon white pepper

Preheat the oven to 500 degrees F.

Place the tomato halves into a baking pan skin side down. Drizzle with the olive oil, salt, and pepper and place in the oven for 30 to 45 minutes, until they are soft and slightly charred. Remove from the oven and keep warm if using immediately or refrigerate. Yield: 8–10 roasted tomatoes

caviar-stuffed eggs

I love taking retro recipes and putting little spins on them that bring them into the present. The addition of anchovy paste to this filling is a nice, salty surprise, and the lumpfish caviar is affordable. Of course, if you can afford to spring for the expensive stuff . . . invite me over!

Gently place the eggs into a large saucepan and cover with cold water. Add the vinegar and place over high heat. Bring to a boil and cook for exactly 5 minutes. Remove the pan from the heat and let it sit an additional 2 minutes. Drain the eggs and run them under cold water. Immediately peel the eggs (see note) and slice them in half the long way. Place the yolks in a mixing bowl and set the whites aside.

Using a fork, mash the yolks well. Add the mayonnaise, anchovy paste, mustard, and pepper and mix well. Spoon the mixture into a pastry bag fitted with a #6 round tip (½-inch diameter).

Set the egg whites out in a row. Into eight of the halves, spoon ¼ teaspoon of black caviar. Into the other eight halves, spoon ½ teaspoon of red caviar. Pipe the egg-yolk filling on top of the caviar so that each resembles a full yolk. Garnish the black caviar stuffed eggs with a small amount of the red caviar and vice versa. Put a small bed of spring mix onto each plate and set one black caviar and one red caviar egg side by side on top. Serve immediately.

COOK'S NOTE: I've found that the combination of adding vinegar to the eggs' cooking water and peeling them while still hot is the best method for removing the shell easily.

Yield: 8 servings
Preparation time: 20 minutes
Cooking time: 5 minutes

8 large eggs

2 tablespoons white vinegar

¾ cup good quality mayonnaise, such as Hellmann's

1 teaspoon anchovy paste

¼ teaspoon dry mustard

¼ teaspoon white pepper

3½-ounce jar black lumpfish caviar

3½-ounce jar red lumpfish caviar

8 cups spring mix lettuce

SPECIAL EQUIPMENT

Pastry bag fitted with #6 round tip

MAKE AHEAD

The eggs are best made day of. Cooked egg whites tend to get rubbery if made ahead and stored in the refrigerator.

stracciatella

Yield: 8–10 servings
Preparation time: 15 minutes
Cooking time: 20 minutes

1 tablespoon olive oil

3 cloves garlic, thinly sliced

6 cups low-sodium chicken broth

2 cups low-sodium beef broth

3 teaspoons kosher salt

4 large eggs

1 tablespoon finely grated Romano cheese, plus additional for serving

1 tablespoon flour

½ teaspoon freshly ground black pepper

4 cups chopped escarole (about ½ head)

SPECIAL EQUIPMENT

Colander

Growing up, this was comfort food in our Italian home. I can remember my mom standing over a big pot on the stove, gently stirring beaten egg into chicken broth. The egg would form long, lacy strands, leaving the broth a clear amber color. Sometimes she'd add greens to the soup and sometimes not, but she always topped it with freshly grated Romano cheese. Either way, when I make it now, I think about the everyday meals that we would all sit down to as a family.

Pour the olive oil into a large saucepan and add the garlic. Place over medium heat and cook, stirring occasionally, until the garlic begins to turn golden, 7 to 10 minutes. Add both broths and 2 teaspoons of the salt and raise the heat to high.

As the broth comes to a boil, beat the eggs together with the tablespoon of Romano, the remaining salt, and the pepper. Lower the heat so that the broth is just simmering, place a colander over the saucepan and pour the egg mixture into the colander. The egg will flow through the colander holes into the soup in an even stream. Remove the colander, stir in the escarole, and simmer for 2 to 3 minutes.

Ladle the soup into bowls and top with grated Romano. This final step will really make the soup, so don't skip it. Serve immediately.

Honey roasted parsnip Bisque

This bisque is destined to become a holiday tradition in our family. I made it last Christmas—both Steve's family and mine were with us for the holiday, and we had 20 for dinner. The earthy, slightly sweet, velvety texture caused everyone at the table to ask for the recipe. I can't think of a more perfect soup for a holiday dinner.

Preheat the oven to 375 degrees F.

Toss the parsnips with the oil, 1 tablespoon of the honey, and 1 teaspoon of the salt, place them on a baking sheet, and put it into the top half of the oven. Roast for 30 minutes, or until the parsnips are a deep golden brown. Because of the honey, they'll tend to burn easily, so make sure to toss often while roasting.

Meanwhile, put 6 cups water into a large pot and place over high heat. Lay a double layer of cheesecloth on a flat surface and place the carrot, onion, parsley, bay leaves, and peppercorns in the center. Tie the cheesecloth up and around the vegetable and herb mix and drop it into the water. Bring to a boil, lower the heat, and simmer for 30 minutes.

Remove the parsnips from the oven and place them immediately into the stock. Add the remaining honey and salt. Simmer an additional 30 minutes until the parsnips are very tender. Remove from the heat, discard the cheesecloth bag, and puree in batches. Return to a saucepan and add the cream and white pepper. Stir well to combine and bring to a simmer. Remove from the heat and serve immediately, or refrigerate until ready to serve.

Yield: 8 cups
Preparation time: 20 minutes
Cooking time: 1 hour

---

2 pounds parsnips, peeled, trimmed, and quartered lengthwise

¼ cup vegetable oil

3 teaspoons kosher salt

1 carrot, peeled, trimmed, and cut in half

1 small onion, unpeeled and halved

1 bunch fresh parsley

2 bay leaves

½ teaspoon black peppercorns

3 tablespoons honey

3 cups heavy cream

2 teaspoons white pepper

SPECIAL EQUIPMENT

Cheesecloth

MAKE AHEAD

The bisque can be made the day before.

moroccan lentil soup with harissa yogurt

Yield: 6–8 servings
Preparation time: 25 minutes
Cooking time: 1 hour

1 pint grape tomatoes

6 tablespoons olive oil

1 tablespoon kosher salt

½ onion, cut into 1-inch dice

2 carrots, peeled, trimmed, and cut into 1-inch pieces

2 cloves garlic, minced

2 cups red lentils

8 cups vegetable broth

2 teaspoons ground cumin

1 teaspoon curry powder

¼ teaspoon cinnamon

Harissa Yogurt, recipe follows

MAKE AHEAD

Soup is best made day of but yogurt can be made up to 3 days in advance.

I grew up eating brown lentils with rice and grated cheese. It was one of those quick dinners that my mom would make when my dad was away. When I moved to New York City, I discovered a small Moroccan restaurant around the corner from my apartment and fell in love with the creamy almost velvety lentil soup they served—worlds different from my mom's lentils. Since I rarely had much money in my pocket, I'd often make that my dinner, along with the fresh, crispy flatbread that they gave you for free!

Preheat the oven to 500 degrees F.

Toss the tomatoes with 3 tablespoons of the olive oil and place on a baking sheet. Sprinkle with 1 teaspoon of the salt and place in the oven until slightly charred, about 20 minutes.

Warm the remaining olive oil in a large saucepan over medium heat and add the onion, carrot, and garlic. Cook until the onion begins to turn translucent, 15 to 20 minutes. Add the lentils and broth and bring to a simmer. Add the remaining salt and the cumin, curry powder, and cinnamon, stir well, and let simmer until the lentils have broken down, 30 to 40 minutes. Stir in the roasted tomatoes and serve topped with a small dollop of the yogurt.

harissa yogurt

2 tablespoons crushed red pepper

1 large garlic clove

1 teaspoon ground cumin

¼ teaspoon ground coriander

Pinch cinnamon

3 tablespoons extra-virgin olive oil

½ cup Greek yogurt, or plain yogurt left to drain overnight in cheesecloth

Put the red pepper, garlic, cumin, and cinnamon into a spice grinder (coffee grinder reserved specifically for spices) and grind until fine. Pour into a small bowl and add 3 tablespoons water and the olive oil. Stir until a paste forms. Add the yogurt and whisk until smooth. Yield: ¾ cup

theme parties

In order for a theme party to be truly unforgettable, you've got to use your imagination! A "beach" theme where the guys wear Hawaiian shirts, and everyone gets plastic leis just doesn't cut it. It's the same party you went to last week, except now the girls are wearing flip-flops. You need to think of ways to cause a stir and create conversation.

Some of my favorite theme parties have included a 1980s fundraiser where everyone had to wear their prom dresses and pastel tuxes, an Oscar party where guests came as a character from one of the nominated movies (we did this in 2002 and re-created the cocktail party menu that Julianne Moore used in *Far From Heaven*), and a grown-up scavenger hunt where guests split into groups and drove all around town causing mayhem and talking their way into obtaining items. The party really soared when all the groups returned for cocktails and war stories.

Of course, you should always match your menu to the event. For a Kentucky Derby Party we had a client who went above and beyond when she contacted Kentucky's governor to ask what he traditionally served at his own derby celebration. We recreated his menu in miniature and passed mini Hot Brown sandwiches and mint juleps to guests who wore fabulous hats and seersucker suits. There may even have been a little wagering, but if you talk to the governor . . . you didn't hear that from me.

simple salad with grape vinaigrette, feta, and walnuts

Yield: 6–8 servings
Preparation Time: 10 minutes

8 cups mesclun greens

Pinch kosher salt

Couple grinds of freshly ground black pepper

8 ounces feta cheese, crumbled

1 cup oven-toasted walnuts

Grape Vinaigrette, recipe follows

MAKE AHEAD

Salad must be made day of but vinaigrette can be made up to 1 week in advance.

This is truly a simple salad. It takes almost no time to prepare, but the grape vinaigrette (which also only takes 5 minutes) really dresses it up. Use it as a first course to impress your friends or just pair it with an herb-grilled chicken breast for a quick healthy meal.

Toss the greens, salt, and pepper together with just enough vinaigrette to coat, about ½ cup. Place them in a decorative bowl or onto individual plates and top with the feta and walnuts. Serve immediately.

grape vinaigrette

1 small shallot, peeled and roughly chopped (about 1 tablespoon)

1 cup seedless red grapes

1 teaspoon Dijon mustard

2 tablespoons champagne vinegar

1 tablespoon honey

1 tablespoon kosher salt

½ teaspoon freshly ground black pepper

1 cup olive oil

Put the shallot and grapes into a food processor and process on high until the grapes liquefy. Add the mustard, vinegar, honey, salt, and pepper and pulse. With the machine running, add the olive oil in a steady stream until the vinaigrette emulsifies. Store in the refrigerator until ready to serve. Yield: 2 cups

Baby Arugula salad with Figs and chèvre Toast

Pictured on page 5

Most people believe arugula is a member of the lettuce family. It's actually an herb, a member of the mustard family, which accounts for its peppery taste. In ancient Roman times it was considered an aphrodisiac. . . . Just throwing that fact out there. Do with it what you will.

Place the shallot in the bowl of a food processor and pulse. Add the balsamic, sugar, and Dijon and pulse. With the machine running, add the olive oil in a steady stream until the vinaigrette emulsifies. Whisk in salt and pepper to taste.

Toss the greens with enough vinaigrette to coat all the leaves. Divide between the eight salad plates and top with the chèvre toasts and figs. Serve immediately.

chèvre Toast

8 slices baguette, cut on the bias, about ½ inch thick

Extra-virgin olive oil

4 ounces chèvre (goat cheese)

8 fresh rosemary sprigs

Kosher salt and freshly ground black pepper

Preheat the oven to 400 degrees F.

Place eight baguette slices on a baking sheet, brush them with a little olive oil and top with the chèvre. Top each with a rosemary sprig, a sprinkle of salt and pepper, and drizzle a tiny bit more olive oil on them. Set the pan in the oven for 10 to 15 minutes. Keep an eye on them—you want the cheese to melt, but you don't want the toasts to burn. Remove from the oven and set aside.

Yield: 8 servings
Preparation time: 15 minutes
Cooking time: 15 minutes

VINAIGRETTE

1 shallot, peeled and coarsely chopped

¼ cup balsamic vinegar

1 tablespoon sugar

1 tablespoon Dijon mustard

1 cup extra-virgin olive oil

SALAD

8 cups baby arugula

Chèvre Toast, recipe follows

8 fresh figs, quartered

MAKE AHEAD

Dressing can be made up to 1 week in advance. Salad must be made day of.

chilled Beets and Asparagus with nasturtiums

Yield: 6–8 servings
Preparation Time: 20 minutes
Cooking Time: 30 minutes

2 bunches baby beets (12–14 beets), peeled and quartered (see note)

Kosher salt

1 bunch asparagus, ends trimmed and cut on the bias into 1-inch pieces.

½ cup chives, cut into 1-inch pieces

10–12 edible nasturtium blossoms (other edible flowers may be substituted)

1 cup water

½ cup orange-blossom water (see note)

1½ cups sugar

1 tablespoon fresh lemon juice

4 ounces crumbly goat cheese

Mixed greens, for serving

Beets are either something you love or hate. I started to appreciate them back in college when a friend much wealthier than I took a group of us out to dinner at the Russian Tea Room on 57th Street. I ordered the borscht, and it was a revelation—cool, creamy, and earthy. Nowadays I love beets and can't wait for the farmer's market in springtime so I can get all the different baby varieties. Unfortunately, I wind up eating them alone in our house because Steve hates them. So don't be like Steve! Try this recipe even if you only like beets a little bit—their earthiness pairs beautifully with the orange blossom glaze, and the nasturtiums add a great touch.

Put the beets in a large saucepan, add enough cold water to cover, and place over medium-high heat until the water comes to a boil. Immediately lower the heat to medium and let the beets cook for about 20 minutes, or just until fork-tender. Run the beets under cold water, then drain them and spread them out on a baking sheet. Using a piece of paper towel, blot the beets to remove as much excess water as possible.

Fill the pot with water again and bring it to a boil. Salt the water liberally and blanch the asparagus by dropping it into the boiling water for 1 minute, then drain and run it under cold water immediately. Drain, blot, and add to the beets.

To make the glaze, in a small saucepan, combine 1 cup water, the orange-blossom water, sugar, and lemon juice. Bring the mixture to a boil, reduce the heat to medium, and simmer until the glaze is reduced by half and has thickened slightly. Toss the glaze with the vegetables and add the chives. Top with the nasturtiums and crumbled goat cheese. Serve on a bed of mixed greens.

COOK'S NOTE: Be sure to wear latex gloves while peeling beets. Otherwise, they'll stain your hands. Orange-blossom water can be found in specialty stores and Middle Eastern markets.

Hearts of Romaine Caesar Salad

Yield: 8 servings
Preparation time: 30 minutes
Cooking time: 18 minutes

CROUTONS

12-inch sourdough boule, cut into 2-inch cubes (you'll have some triangles mixed in there as well)

2 cloves garlic, minced

1 teaspoon kosher salt

2 teaspoons freshly ground black pepper

4 tablespoons (½ stick) unsalted butter, melted

¼ cup olive oil

1 tablespoon chopped fresh parsley

SALAD

4 romaine hearts, split lengthwise

Caesar Dressing, recipe follows

Shaved Parmesan cheese

Freshly ground black pepper

MAKE AHEAD

Croutons are best made day of, but dressing can be made up to 1 week in advance.

Two things are different about this Caesar salad: The presentation is really eye-catching, and the dressing is what I like to call "kicky." It's got a lot of robust flavors going on, and the hot sauce gives it just enough bite at the end to make you want another bite . . . or four.

Preheat the oven to 375 degrees F.

Place the sourdough cubes into a large bowl along with the garlic, salt, and pepper. Add the butter and olive oil and toss quickly.

Arrange the croutons on a baking sheet and place them in the top half of the oven for 15 to 18 minutes, or until golden. Remove, return them to the bowl, and toss with the parsley. Let cool.

Place half a romaine heart onto each plate and drizzle it with 2 tablespoons dressing. Top with generous amounts of shaved Parmesan and pepper. Add three croutons per plate and serve immediately.

caesar Dressing

4 cloves garlic

2 teaspoons anchovy paste

1 teaspoon kosher salt

2 teaspoons dry mustard

¼ cup fresh lemon juice

1 tablespoon hot sauce, such as Tabasco

¾ cup extra-virgin olive oil

¾ cup good quality mayonnaise, such as Hellmann's

Put the garlic, anchovy paste, and salt into the bowl of a food processor and pulse until the garlic is minced. Add the mustard, lemon juice, and hot sauce and run the processor to mix well. With the machine running, add the olive oil in a steady stream. Pour into a bowl and gently whisk in the mayonnaise. Yield: 2 cups

iceberg wedge with Green Goddess Dressing

Iceberg lettuce sort of fell into obscurity back in the 1980s. It was ridiculed as being pedestrian, suburban, and totally unhip. I'm glad that it's finding its way back into favor. I have to say, I'm a fan of its big crunch, and paired with our version of the 1920s' classic green goddess dressing, this salad is a retro dream.

Roast the peppers over an open flame, turning to blacken all the sides. (Alternatively, blacken them under the broiler.) Place them in the paper bag and close it tightly. When cool enough to handle, peel away the skin and rinse the pepper under cool water. Seed the peppers.

Put the roasted peppers into a blender, along with the remaining ingredients. Blend until smooth. Pour into a plastic squeeze bottle and chill until ready to use.

Cut the head of lettuce into eight equal wedges. Squeeze a thin zigzag pattern of pepper coulis onto each serving plate. Place a wedge of lettuce on top and top with 2 to 3 tablespoons of dressing. Sprinkle chives over the salad and serve immediately.

Green Goddess Dressing

2 cloves garlic, crushed

1 cup chopped flat-leaf parsley, packed

½ cup chopped basil leaves, packed

2 tablespoons chopped fresh dill

2 tablespoons chopped chives

1 tablespoon fresh lemon juice

2 teaspoons anchovy paste

1 cup good-quality mayonnaise, such as Hellmann's

¼ teaspoon white pepper

Put all the ingredients into a blender or food processor and pulse on high until smooth and creamy. Refrigerate until ready to serve. Yield: 1¾ cups

---

Yield: 8 servings
Preparation time: 30 minutes

RED PEPPER COULIS

4 red bell peppers

2 cloves garlic, minced

¼ cup extra-virgin olive oil

1 teaspoon kosher salt

½ teaspoon white pepper

SALAD

1 large head iceberg lettuce

Green Goddess Dressing, recipe follows

Chopped chives, for garnish

SPECIAL EQUIPMENT

Squeeze bottle

Brown-paper bag

MAKE AHEAD

Red Pepper Coulis and dressing can be made the day before.

Herb Braised Bosc Pears with Gorgonzola and Frizzled Prosciutto

Yield: 8 servings
Preparation time: 25 minutes
Cooking time: 20 minutes

4 cups hearty red wine,
such as Cabernet

¾ cup honey

1 bunch fresh thyme

3 sprigs fresh rosemary

2 sprigs fresh sage

2 sprigs fresh oregano

1 bunch fresh parsley

2 teaspoons kosher salt

1 tablespoon black peppercorns

4 Bosc pears, halved and
seeded

8 ounces Gorgonzola,
crumbled

8 ounces cream cheese

2 tablespoons brandy

Vegetable oil, for frying

8 thin slices prosciutto

2 large bunches frisée, washed
and spun dry

Pomegranate syrup, for
serving (see note)

Freshly cracked black pepper,
for serving

I created this starter for a gala benefit at Chicago's now-defunct Marshall Field's. Steve and I were there along with at least twenty of the city's top chefs, and as we waited behind the scenes, we critically eyed one another's food. We walked away from our cart for a minute and returned to hear a chef scoffing at our frizzled prosciutto. How can you scoff at crunchy saltiness? Especially when it's paired with the creamy sharpness of Gorgonzola and the herbal sweetness of a braised pear? Who knows . . . maybe he just had cart envy.

Put the wine, honey, herbs, salt, and pepper in a large saucepan and bring to a simmer. Add the pears, cover tightly and reduce the heat to low. Simmer for 20 minutes, until the pears are fork-tender. Remove them from the liquid, let cool, and refrigerate until ready to use. Discard liquid.

Cream the Gorgonzola and cream cheese together until smooth. Add the brandy and mix until well combined. Refrigerate until ready to use.

Pour 1 inch of vegetable oil into a small saucepan and place over medium heat for 2 minutes. Cook the prosciutto, one slice at a time, until frizzled and golden brown, 1–2 minutes. (When the prosciutto hits the hot oil it will shrink and crumple—don't worry—that's normal.). Remove to a paper towel to drain.

When ready to serve the dish, divide the frisée between serving plates and place a pear half on each plate. Fill the hollow in the pear half with the Gorgonzola mix and place a piece of frizzled prosciutto into each Gorgonzola mound. Drizzle the plate with pomegranate syrup and sprinkle with freshly cracked black pepper.

COOK'S NOTE: You can find pomegrante syrup in in gourmet shops and Whole Foods markets

MAKE AHEAD: Pears can be poached and cheese mixture can be made the day before.

pear waldorf

The original Waldorf salad was created at the turn of the last century by the maître d' of the Waldorf-Astoria in New York City. Over the years, it's come in and out of fashion and gone through various incarnations. This is my version, using pears instead of the traditional apples. I've chosen three different types for their varying tastes and textures and paired them with sweet-tart dried cherries and crunchy toasted hazelnuts. It makes a great starter and can also be the feature of a luncheon if you toss in some shredded, poached chicken breast.

Put the mayonnaise, lemon juice, honey, salt and pepper into a large mixing bowl and whisk to combine.

Toss the pears and ¼ cup of the cherries with the dressing until well coated.

Place a leaf of lettuce onto each plate and mound a small amount of pear salad on each leaf. Garnish with the remaining cherries and hazelnuts. Serve immediately.

Yield: 6–8 servings
Preparation time: 15 minutes

¼ cup good-quality mayonnaise, such as Hellmann's

2 tablespoons fresh lemon juice

1 teaspoon honey

1 teaspoon kosher salt

⅛ teaspoon white pepper

1 Anjou pear, cored and sliced ¼ inch thick

1 red pear, cored and sliced ¼ inch thick

1 Asian pear, cored and sliced ¼ inch thick

2 celery ribs, sliced on the bias ¼ inch thick

½ cup dried cherries

8 large, beautiful red lettuce leaves

½ cup toasted hazelnuts, for garnish

musical chairs

There seems to be an underlying fear that runs through our family gatherings that someone will be left without a seat. To combat this possibility, our relatives line the walls with every available chair in the house. Straight-backed dining room chairs stand stiffly next to rockers, whose backs are planted against the same wall as the kitchen chairs and an occasional ottoman. This lends an eerie "Red Rover, Red Rover" feel to the space. People tend to lurk around the edges of the living room, unsure if they've accidentally wandered into a game of dodge ball.

It's fine to utilize your dining room or kitchen chairs for extra seating, but place them in comfortable groups to encourage conversation. I promise you, your guests would all prefer to face each other rather than a vast no-man's-land in the center of the room. I'm no interior designer, but I'm thinking that "high school dance" is not the best model when you're setting up a room.

main Dishes

During those early days in Chicago, two of our favorite clients were Ken Bode, then dean of Northwestern University's Medill School of Journalism, and his wife, Margot. Guest speakers would deliver a speech on campus, and a select group would gather at the Bodes' for a comfortable meal and rehashing of the evening. Margot is a terrific hostess who understands the power of background music at an event, and her choice of Creedence Clearwater Revival or Janis Joplin would take the air out of any stuffed shirt and put everyone on an even playing field.

Their menu choices reflected the comfort level they wanted to achieve as well. We'd offer hearty one-pot favorites like Crawfish Étouffée; Chicken, Sausage, and Shrimp Stew; and garlic-studded roasts. We'd always put out a few hot sauces from Ken's collection and finish off with Margot's favorite peach upside down cake before moving to the sunroom for cordials.

Not long after the Monica Lewinsky scandal hit its peak, we were asked to do a small dinner party where Kenneth Starr was the guest of honor. After enjoying the conversation at a recent dinner hosted for President Clinton's press secretary, Mike McCurry, as well as one for Jesse Jackson Jr., (and after advising Margot against the "blue dress" she was threatening to wear), I knew this was one meal that we'd be talking about for a while.

Dan and I were finishing preparations on the hors d'oeuvres. We often didn't have time to eat during these events, so we'd eat what we could on the fly. As soon as I popped an oversized artichoke fritter in my mouth, the host surprised us by bringing Ken Starr in the back door and directly into the kitchen where Dan and I stood.

Mr. Starr bounded in, all smiles and energy, grabbed my hand, and introduced himself. I was completely caught off guard as I had expected to be interrogated or at least served a summons. "So, you're preparing the food tonight?" he asked. I tried frantically to finish chewing the fritter I had stuffed in my mouth, but apparently I had grabbed one the size of a Wiffle ball. "No," I choked, "not preparing . . . just eating."

As I continued in my effort to work through this immense fritter, Mr. Starr chatted away, all the while rigorously shaking my hand. He asked me about The Hearty Boys and was very kind and gracious, but this guy would simply not let go of my hand. I chewed and shook, shook and chewed, chewed and shook. . . .

I learn something at each party we throw but I really hit the knowledge jackpot that night. I now know that while it's a good idea to make sure you grab a bite early on if you're afraid you'll be too busy hosting, try to remember what "bite-sized" means when assembling hors d'oeuvres, and that apparently, you can't be subpoenaed with your mouth full.

Lingonberry-stuffed meatballs with Tarragon Butter sauce

Yield: serves 8
Preparation time: 30 minutes
Cooking time: 45 minutes

2½ pounds ground beef

1½ pounds ground veal

1 small yellow onion, minced

4 sprigs fresh tarragon, leaves stripped and coarsely chopped

4 teaspoons herbes de Provence

4 teaspoons kosher salt

2½ teaspoons white pepper

8 eggs

4 cups Panko (see note)

⅓ cup dried cranberries

⅓ cup raisins

¾ cup dry vermouth

3 tablespoons lingonberry sauce or cranberry sauce

Vegetable oil

Tarragon Butter Sauce, recipe follows

When we found out that we'd been picked for *The Next Food Network Star*, we immediately began to panic about the "challenges" that would face us. We had no idea what to expect. We were just taking a stab in the dark when we decided to do a market-basket challenge with HB's executive chef, Joncarl Lachman. Our sous-chef Terry went to the store and bought a bunch of food that he put into a covered basket. Once the groceries were uncovered, we would have an hour to create a meal using all the ingredients.

Terry whipped the towel off that basket, and all I could think was, "Oh, #%*&! What am I going to do with ground veal?" Not wanting to go the meatloaf route (which just seemed too obvious) I came up with this recipe, which is now on HB's menu. The lingonberry stuffing is like a little surprise when you cut into the meatball!

Put the beef, veal, onion, tarragon, herbes de Provence, salt, and pepper into a large mixing bowl. Lightly beat the eggs and pour them over the meat. Mix well using your hands (it's the best way to make meatballs). Add 2 cups of the bread crumbs and mix well. Set aside.

Put the cranberries, raisins, and vermouth in a small saucepan over medium heat and bring to a simmer. Cook the mix until the fruits are nice and plump about 5 minutes. Remove from the heat, drain and discard the liquid, and put the fruits in a food processor along with the lingonberry sauce. Pulse until a paste forms. Set aside.

Form the meat mixture into 16 large balls, between 4 and 5 ounces each. Make a well in the center of each ball with your thumb and fill it with 1 heaping teaspoon of the fruit mixture. Push the meat back over the fruit, making sure to seal the hole, then refrigerate for at least 30 minutes or overnight.

When you are ready to cook the meatballs, preheat the oven to 375 degrees F.

Pour 3 inches of vegetable oil into a large, deep-sided skillet and place it over medium heat for 7 to 10 minutes. Test the oil by dropping a bread cube into it. If the cube browns quickly, the oil is ready. Remove the meatballs from the refrigerator and roll them in the remaining bread crumbs. Carefully place them

Pictured on page 91

into the skillet four at a time. Keep a close watch on them, making sure to turn them so they get golden brown on all sides. Remove with a slotted spoon and place on a paper towel–lined plate to drain.

When all the meatballs are cooked, arrange them on a baking sheet and place them in the oven for 20 minutes. Remove, top with Tarragon Butter Sauce, and serve immediately.

COOK'S NOTE: Japanese breadcrumbs, also known as Panko, can be found in specialty stores and Asian markets.

tarragon butter sauce

1 small bunch fresh tarragon

1 small carrot

1 plum tomato, halved

1 celery rib

2 teaspoons kosher salt

1 tablespoon finely chopped fresh tarragon

12 tablespoons (1½ sticks) unsalted butter, chilled and cut into bits

Freshly ground black pepper

Place a sprig of tarragon, the carrot, tomato, celery, and salt into a medium-sized pot along with 2 cups water and place over medium-high heat. Bring to a boil and reduce heat. Let simmer until the mix is reduced by half. Strain the stock, discarding the solids, and return it to the heat to reduce it to ½ cup.

Chop enough tarragon leaves to make 1 tablespoon, then add the tarragon and whisk in the butter a tablespoon at a time, making sure it is incorporated before adding more. Taste and season with additional salt and some pepper, if desired. Pour over meatballs immediately. Yield: 1 cup

MAKE AHEAD

The meatballs can be formed the day before and cooked the day of.

Joncarl's Blackened Pork Chop with smoked oyster stuffing

Yield: 8 servings
Preparation time: 20 minutes
Cooking time: 20 minutes

½ cup (1 stick) unsalted butter

1 large onion, cut into ½-inch dice

2 celery ribs, cut into ½-inch dice

2 teaspoons kosher salt

2 teaspoons freshly ground black pepper

8 slices pumpernickel bread, cut into 1-inch squares

4 eggs, lightly beaten

Two 3¾-ounce cans roughly chopped smoked oysters

8 double-cut pork chops

Cajun spices to taste

1 cup vegetable oil

Kosher salt and pepper to taste

MAKE AHEAD

Stuffing can be made the day before. Chops must be filled and cooked directly before serving.

Before we opened HB, our executive chef, Joncarl, and I would occasionally give cooking classes that focused on parties—anything from hors d'oeuvres to dinner to dessert parties. We would ply the small hands-on groups with wine upon arrival, which served to break the ice. We'd all cook together and then sit down to eat what we'd made. By the time class was over, phone numbers had been exchanged and friends had been made. Joncarl created this recipe for one of those classes. It was such a hit that when the restaurant opened, we featured it on the menu.

Preheat the oven to 350 degrees F.

To make the stuffing, melt the butter in a skillet over medium heat. Add the onion, celery, salt, and pepper and cook 5 to 7 minutes until the vegetables are slightly translucent.

Place the bread in a mixing bowl. Add the eggs to the bread along with the onion and celery mixture and smoked oysters.

When you are ready to prepare the dish, season the pork chops with the Cajun spices. (Remember, the more you use, the spicier the chop will be.)

Pour ½ cup of the oil into a large skillet and place it over high heat until the oil begins to smoke. Sear the pork chops two at a time, placing them carefully into the hot oil to avoid spattering. Remove and set aside when a crust is formed. Follow with the remaining pork chops, adding more oil as needed.

When the chops are cool enough to touch, cut a slit down the middle and fill the cavity with some of the stuffing.

Place the stuffed chops in the oven. Roast for about 20 minutes, or until the thickest part of the pork registers 130 degrees F on an instant-read thermometer.

Remove the chops from the oven, cover them with foil, and allow them to rest for 10 minutes before serving.

pepper-encrusted rack of lamb with Madagascar green peppercorn sauce

Yield: 8 servings
Preparation time: 10 minutes
Cooking time: 30 minutes

4 French racks of lamb, trimmed and cleaned (see note)

1 tablespoon kosher salt

½ cup black peppercorns, coarsely ground

Vegetable oil

Madagascar Green Peppercorn Sauce, recipe follows

I'll never forget the first time I prepared rack of lamb professionally. I cheffed a party at an enormous apartment in the Dakota in New York City. (This is the building John Lennon once lived in.) I wasn't supposed to be in charge—the head of the company, my dear friend Francine Maroukian, had come down sick that day and wasn't able to get out of bed, so she sent me.

It was the very first party I'd handled alone, so I was a wreck. I kept asking the waiter to count the guests—as soon as the 20th walked through the front door, I would start the lamb. It got later . . . and later . . . and later, and I got more . . . and more . . . and more panicked. The waiter kept telling me that there were only 19 guests in the living room. Well yeah, there were 19 guests—plus the host—which equaled 20.

Once I discovered his gaffe, peeled myself off the ceiling, and stopped banging his head against the stove (only in my mind), I found out how quickly and easily rack of lamb is prepared. I had dinner on the table within 20 minutes.

Preheat the oven to 425 degrees F.

Sprinkle the lamb liberally on all sides with the salt and pepper.

Pour a thin layer of vegetable oil into a large skillet and place over high heat until the oil begins to smoke, 1 to 2 minutes. Working in batches, place the racks into the skillet. Sear for 1 minute per side, remove, and put on a baking sheet.

Put the lamb into the oven and cook 12 minutes for rare, 15 minutes for medium rare. Remove from the oven and let rest 5 minutes before slicing. Using a sharp knife, cut each rack in half. Place the meat on the plates, spoon the peppercorn sauce over it, and serve.

COOK'S NOTE: French rack of lamb simply means that the excess fat has been removed from the bones and that they've been cleaned up before cooking. Ask your butcher to French them to save yourself time.

madagascar green peppercorn sauce

2 plum tomatoes, halved

3 shallots

1 carrot split

1 bunch fresh parsley

4 cups beef stock

1 cup red wine

¾ cup heavy cream

2 tablespoons green peppercorns in brine

Place the first five ingredients in a large saucepan and bring to a boil. Reduce the heat to low and let simmer until reduced by half.

Strain the sauce, discard the solids, and return it to the pan. Add the wine and peppercorns. Reduce by half again.

Whisk in the heavy cream, return the sauce to a boil, reduce the heat, and let simmer until slightly thickened, about 5 minutes. Serve immediately with the lamb or refrigerate until serving. Yield: 2 cups

help!

I have found that when people ask, "Can I help?" they usually mean it. Early birds especially enjoy the opportunity to have a task. To take advantage of this, organize your preparations so that your last-minute details can be delegated. For example, have your cheese platter set to go out, but leave the garnishing till the last minute. Then point your helper toward the fridge with instructions about how to decorate the platter with nuts and dried fruits. Have helpers place your veggie basket on the buffet and pour your dips into bowls so you can continue with the big-picture preparations. Trust me, it makes people happy to feel helpful. So, be altruistic and give someone else your work!

MAKE AHEAD

Peppercorn sauce can be made the day before and reheated.

cider-braised pork roast stuffed with figs and apricots

When autumn comes around, I always want to eat pork roast. I don't know why, but to me, pork is the quintessential fall meat! Braising it in apple cider and adding the dried fruits make it just about the season's perfect main course.

Preheat the oven to 300 degrees F.

Warm 3 tablespoons of the vegetable oil in a large skillet over medium heat. Add the onion and cook until translucent, about 10 minutes. Add the dried fruit, 1 teaspoon of the salt, the peppercorns, caraway seeds, and thyme sprigs. Raise the heat to high and add the brandy. Touch a match to the pan in order to flame the brandy. (Be careful with this step—the flame will be vigorous.) Allow the flame to go out on its own, lower the heat, and let the mixture simmer until almost dry, about 5 minutes.

Lay the pork loin out on a flat surface and sprinkle with salt. Spoon the fruit mixture onto the center of the loin, working from one end to the other. Roll the loin around the filling so it looks like it did when uncut. Tie with butcher's string.

Put the remaining vegetable oil into a large skillet and heat it over high heat for 2 minutes. Put the roast into the skillet. Sear on all sides for 1 minute and remove to a roasting pan. Add the cider, bay leaves, cloves, thyme and remaining salt to the skillet. Bring to a boil to deglaze the pan, making sure to stir up any brown bits from the bottom.

Pour the liquid over the roast, cover it with foil, and place it in the oven. Braise for 3½ hours, turning once during the cooking process. Remove the roast from the pan and allow to sit for 15 minutes before slicing.

To make gravy, pour 1 cup of the braising liquid into a saucepan, using a strainer to make sure there are no solids. Skim as much of the fat from the top as possible, bring the liquid to a boil, and whisk in the butter. Correct seasonings and serve immediately with the pork.

Yield: 6–8 servings
Preparation time: 40 minutes
Cooking time: 3½ hours

6 tablespoons vegetable oil

1 Spanish onion, thinly sliced

½ cup chopped dried Mission figs

½ cup chopped dried apricots

3 teaspoons kosher salt

½ teaspoon pink peppercorns

½ teaspoon caraway seeds

4 sprigs fresh thyme

¼ cup brandy

1 pork loin, 2½–3 pounds, butterflied

4 cups unfiltered apple cider

5 bay leaves

8 cloves

1 bunch fresh thyme

½ cup (1 stick) unsalted butter, cut into bits

SPECIAL EQUIPMENT

Butcher's string

Braised short ribs with Merlot reduction

Yield: 8 servings
Preparation time: 30 minutes
Cooking time: 4 hours

¼ cup vegetable oil

10 pounds beef short ribs
(about 24 ribs)

Kosher salt and freshly ground
black pepper

4 celery ribs

2 carrots, split lengthwise

3 cloves garlic, crushed

2 plum tomatoes, halved

12 juniper berries, crushed

2 teaspoons black peppercorns

Two 14-ounce cans low-sodium
beef broth

3 cups Merlot

2 tablespoons unsalted butter,
at room temperature

1 tablespoon flour

SPECIAL EQUIPMENT

Roasting pan with cover

Short ribs used to be a bargain because they can be tough and somewhat fatty. Go to the store nowadays, though, and you'll be surprised at how pricey they've become. That's because restaurant chefs discovered them and started educating people about how delicious they are if prepared properly. The secret's in the slow cooking and their sauce. Try these ribs, and I guarantee you'll be hooked.

Preheat the oven to 300 degrees F.

Warm the oil in a large skillet over medium-high heat for 3 minutes. Meanwhile, season the ribs well with salt and pepper on both sides. Put eight ribs into the skillet and sear for 2 minutes per side, or until a golden crust has formed. Transfer to a roasting pan and repeat with the remaining ribs.

Add the celery, carrots, and garlic to the skillet and cook, shaking occasionally, until the veggies are lightly brown, 3 to 5 minutes. Remove the veggies, drain off the excess oil, leaving about 2 tablespoons in the skillet, and return to the heat. Put the veggies back in the skillet, along with the tomatoes, juniper berries, peppercorns, broth, and 2 cups of the wine. Bring the mixture to a boil, then carefully pour it over the ribs. Cover the roasting pan and place it in the oven for 3 hours.

Remove the pan from the oven and place the ribs on a serving platter. Set aside until cool enough to handle. Strain the braising liquid into a saucepan, skim as much of the grease from the top as possible, and discard the solids. Place the saucepan over high heat, add the remaining cup of wine, and bring to a boil. Reduce the heat to medium and reduce the liquid to 2 cups.

Once the ribs are cool enough to handle, remove the meat from the bone (it should slide right off). Trim the meat pieces so that they're rectangular and return them to the roasting pan.

In a small bowl, using a small spoon, mix the butter and flour together until a paste forms. Bring the reduced liquid back to a rapid simmer and slowly add the butter mixture to it, whisking as you go. The sauce will thicken nicely. Pour the Merlot reduction over the ribs and put them back in the oven for 20 minutes.

To serve, place two ribs on each plate and top with the Merlot reduction.

beef and veal stifado

Possibly one of the best trips Steve and I ever took was to Athens and the Greek islands. It was quite a few years ago, and we were on a pretty tight budget, so we packed big backpacks and stayed in cheap hotels, saving the bulk of our money for food and drink. We drank Greek wine and ate mezethes in the shadow of the Parthenon. On Mykonos, we stumbled across a taverna that served a stupendous stifado, or meat stew.

Now, since the streets of Mykonos were designed to confuse ancient pirates with their twists and turns, we were never able to find the restaurant again. (The amount of wine might have had something to do with it, as well.) The flavors of the dish continued to haunt me, though, so I've tried to re-create it here, using a combination of beef and veal. Try it for a homey, intimate dinner party or increase the recipe to serve on a large buffet—either way, the intense flavors will leave you wanting more.

Preheat the oven to 350 degrees F.

Warm ¼ cup of the oil in a large skillet over medium-high heat for 2 to 3 minutes. Season the flour liberally with salt and pepper, mix well, and sprinkle all but 3 tablespoons of it onto a large plate.

Dredge the beef and veal in the flour mixture and place it in the skillet in batches, making sure not to crowd the pan. When the meat is brown on all sides, transfer it to a large roasting pan. Add more oil to the skillet as needed when cooking the meat.

When all the meat has been browned, heat ¼ cup of the olive oil in the pan and add the onion, shallots, garlic, and rosemary. Cook until the onion slices begin to soften, about 10 minutes. Sprinkle on the reserved flour and stir to coat. Add the remaining ingredients and simmer for about 10 minutes—the sauce will thicken.

Pour the sauce over the meat in the roasting pan and stir to combine. Cover the pan and place it in the oven for 3 hours, stirring once every hour so the meat won't stick. Serve over noodles or roasted potatoes, topped with the crumbled feta.

Yield: 8–10 servings
Preparation time: 25 minutes
Cooking time: 3½ hours

About ¾ cup olive oil

1 cup all-purpose flour

Kosher salt and freshly ground black pepper

2 pounds cubed beef stew meat

2 pounds cubed veal stew meat

1 large onion, cut into ½-inch slices

2 cups shallots, peeled and quartered

6 large cloves garlic, crushed

3 rosemary sprigs, each about 6 inches long

2 cups Cabernet

Two 28-ounce cans diced tomatoes with juice

3 cinnamon sticks

2 tablespoons red wine vinegar

2 tablespoons capers

Buttered egg noodles or Oven-roasted Yukon Gold Potatoes (see page 128), for serving

6 ounces Greek feta cheese, crumbled, for serving

middle eastern beef kebabs

Yield: 8 servings
Preparation time: 40 minutes
Cooking time: 12 minutes

1 green bell pepper, seeded
and cut into 8 chunks

2 pounds beef tenderloin,
trimmed and cut into 16 cubes

4 preserved lemons, halved
(see note)

1 red onion, peeled and cut
into chunks

1 red bell pepper, seeded and
cut into 8 chunks

8 white mushrooms, wiped
clean and stems trimmed

2 cloves garlic, chopped

2 tablespoons chopped
flat-leaf parsley

2 teaspoons dried oregano

2 teaspoons onion powder

1 teaspoon curry powder

1 teaspoon cinnamon

1 tablespoon kosher salt

2 teaspoons freshly ground
black pepper

1 cup olive oil

Cucumber Yogurt Sauce,
recipe follows

SPECIAL EQUIPMENT

Eight 10-inch skewers, soaked
in water for 30 minutes

I know that when you read this recipe you're going to say, "Tenderloin on a kebab? What is he—nuts?" The great thing about using this more expensive cut of meat is that there's no extra work involved—it's so tender that it doesn't need to be marinated and tenderized before skewering.

Thread a piece of green pepper onto the skewer. Follow it with a cube of beef, then half of a preserved lemon, a couple of pieces of onion, another piece of beef, and a piece of red pepper, then cap the kebab with a mushroom. Repeat the process with the rest of the skewers. Arrange the kebabs in one layer in a roasting pan and set aside.

Place the remaining ingredients in a medium-sized bowl and whisk until well incorporated. Pour the mixture over the kebabs and refrigerate for 1 hour.

Fire up your grill (whether you use a gas grill or charcoal, make sure it's nice and hot—don't rush it) Place the kebabs on the grill and cook 3 minutes per side. Serve warm or at room temperature, accompanied by the yogurt sauce.

COOK'S NOTE: Tangy, briny preserved lemons can be found in specialty food stores and Middle Eastern markets

cucumber yogurt sauce

1 cup Greek yogurt

½ cucumber, unpeeled, seeded
and diced

1 tablespoon diced onion

Zest of 1 lemon

Pinch dried mint

Kosher salt and freshly ground
black pepper to taste

Place all the ingredients into the bowl of a food processor and pulse until slightly chunky. Serve in a decorative bowl on the side. Yield: 1½ cups

MAKE AHEAD: Sauce can be made up to 2 days in advance.

Bacon and Blue cheese "Matt Loaf"

Yield: 6–8 servings
Preparation time: 20 minutes
Cooking time: 1 hour 15 minutes

8 ounces bacon, cut into 1-inch dice, plus 5 whole slices for topping the loaf

1 small onion, diced

3 pounds ground beef

3 eggs

1 cup good quality mayonnaise, such as Hellmann's

1 cup seasoned bread crumbs

12 ounces blue cheese, crumbled

3 tablespoons chopped fresh parsley

1 teaspoon kosher salt

1 teaspoon freshly ground black pepper

MAKE AHEAD

Loaf is best made day of but can be made day before and reheated.

When we first opened our gourmet take away shop, our friend Matt worked with us both in the kitchen and behind the counter. Although he was a divinity student and not interested in making food his career, he made a mean meatloaf! He used lots of salty, crispy bacon and sharp, tangy blue cheese. It flew out the door every time he made it. Here's the recipe—it's killer!

Preheat the oven to 375 degrees F.

Cook the diced bacon a skillet over high heat, stirring frequently, until it is crisp. Transfer it to a paper towel–lined plate. Pour off all but a couple of tablespoons of the bacon fat, reduce the heat to medium, and add the onion to the pan. Cook, stirring occasionally, until the onion is translucent, about 10 minutes. Remove from the heat and let cool for 5 minutes.

Meanwhile, put the ground beef, eggs, mayonnaise, bread crumbs, blue cheese, parsley, salt, and pepper into a large bowl. Add the cooked bacon and onions and stir by hand until everything is well combined. Don't overwork the mixture or the meat loaf will be mealy.

Transfer the mixture to a large baking dish and pat it into a loaf roughly 12 by 7 by 2 inches. Arrange the bacon slices over the top of the loaf and place it into the top half of the oven for 1 hour and 15 minutes, or until an instant-read thermometer inserted into the thickest part registers 140 degrees F. Remove the meat loaf from the oven and let sit for 15 minutes before slicing.

chicken, sausage, and shrimp stew

The combination of poultry, pork, and seafood might seem a little odd at first but take a second and think about paella. That traditional Spanish dish often uses the same combination for a stunning mix of flavors. Add the fresh fennel and orange zest and the whole dish really pops. Serve it over Oven-Roasted Yukon Gold Potatoes (see page 128) for a real treat.

Melt 6 tablespoons of the butter in a large, heavy bottomed stockpot over medium heat. Just before the butter begins to brown, add the chicken. Season with a little salt and pepper and cook until browned on all sides, about 8 minutes. Add the andouille and cook for 2 more minutes. Transfer the meat to a large dish and set aside.

Melt the remaining butter in the same stockpot. Add the onion, garlic, carrots, fennel, thyme, and bay leaves and cook over medium heat until the onion turns translucent, about 20 minutes.

As the vegetables cook, pour the chicken stock into a large saucepan. Place over medium heat and bring to a simmer. Reduce heat to low.

Add the orange zest and reserved meats with juices to the vegetable mixture. Mix well. Sprinkle on the flour and stir to coat the vegetables and meat. Cook for 2 minutes. Add the wine and stir. The mixture will thicken immediately. Add the warm chicken stock to the pot 1 cup at a time, stirring as the stock is added. Once all of the stock has been used, add the shrimp and bring the stew to a simmer and let it cook for 20 minutes. Ladle into bowls and serve.

Yield: 6–8 servings
Preparation time: 20 minutes
Cooking time: 1 hour

10 tablespoons unsalted butter

2 pounds boneless chicken thigh meat, cut into 2-inch chunks

Kosher salt and freshly ground black pepper to taste

8 ounces andouille sausage, sliced ½ inch thick

½ large onion, cut into 1-inch dice

2 cloves garlic, minced

2 carrots, cut into ½-inch coins

1 small fennel bulb, trimmed and sliced ½ inch thick

2 sprigs fresh thyme

2 bay leaves

5 cups chicken stock

Zest of 1 orange

½ cup all-purpose flour

¼ cup Chardonnay

1 pound large shrimp (26–30 count), peeled and deveined

chicken pot pie

Yield: 6–8 servings
Preparation time: 1 hour
Baking time: 45 minutes

4 pounds chicken thighs and legs

Kosher salt

Freshly ground black pepper

3–4 small red potatoes, cut into 1-inch dice (about 2 cups)

½ cup (1 stick) unsalted butter

¼ cup vegetable oil

1 Spanish onion, cut into ½-inch dice

8 medium carrots cut into ½-inch dice

4 medium parsnips cut into ½-inch dice

1 sprig rosemary

½ cup all-purpose flour, plus additional for the work surface

3 cups low-sodium chicken broth

1 tablespoon fresh basil, chopped

2 tablespoons chopped fresh parsley

1 cup frozen corn

1 cup frozen peas

Biscuit Topping, recipe follows

1 egg, beaten for egg wash

Remember the frozen pot pies in little bitty pie tins that your mom used to buy? Well, this ain't that! The moist, dark chicken meat combined with the fresh vegetables and herbs are capped by a rich biscuit topping. This recipe has so much going on that it's going to quickly become your favorite chicken pot pie. And if you insist, you can cook individual servings in ramekins—or bitty tins.

Preheat the oven to 400 degrees F.

Put the chicken on a baking sheet, season with salt and pepper to taste, and bake in the top half of the oven for 30 minutes. When the chicken is done, remove it from the oven and let it sit until cool enough to handle. Lower the oven temperature to 375 degrees F. Remove the skin from the chicken and discard it. Pull all the meat from the bones and shred it. Set aside.

Put the potatoes into a large saucepan and cover with water. Add 1 teaspoon of salt and set over high heat. Bring to a boil, lower the heat slightly, and cook until the potatoes are fork-tender, about 20 minutes. Drain and set aside.

Warm the butter and vegetable oil in a large pot over medium heat. Add the onion, carrots, parsnips, and rosemary and cook, stirring occasionally, until the onion is translucent, about 20 minutes. Add the shredded chicken, sprinkle on the flour, and stir to coat everything well. Add the chicken broth 1 cup at a time, stirring well as you go. The sauce will thicken as the broth is added. Add the basil, parsley, potatoes, corn, peas, and 1 teaspoon each of salt and pepper, then lower the heat and simmer for 10 minutes. Pour the mixture into a 10-by-12-inch baking dish (see note).

Liberally flour a work surface and place the biscuit dough on the flour. Pat the dough out to a ½-inch thickness, making sure it's large enough to cover the whole surface of the pie. Lift it onto the baking dish and trim as needed. Brush with the egg wash.

Place the pot pie onto a baking sheet to catch any drips and put it in the top half of the oven. Bake for 35 to 45 minutes, until the biscuit topping is golden and firm to the touch and the filling is bubbling. Remove the pot pie from the oven and let sit for 15 minutes before serving.

COOK'S NOTE: A decorative oven-safe ceramic dish is best, since the pot pie goes from oven to table.

Biscuit Topping

Try these on their own as well. Just cut them out with a biscuit cutter. They're killer served warm and slathered with butter.

4 cups all purpose flour

2 tablespoons baking powder

2 teaspoons kosher salt

2 teaspoons freshly ground black pepper

1 tablespoon chopped fresh dill

¾ cup (1½ sticks) butter, chilled and cut into bits

1¾ cups heavy cream, chilled

Put the flour, baking powder, salt, pepper, and dill in the bowl of a food processor and pulse to combine. Add the butter and process until the mixture is crumbly. Transfer to a bowl and add the cream. Mix with a wooden spoon until all the flour is combined. Turn out onto a floured surface and knead just until a ball forms. Wrap in plastic and store in the refrigerator until ready to use.

MAKE AHEAD

Filling can be made 2 days in advance and refrigerated in the baking dish. Biscuit topping should be prepared and baked day of.

balsamic mushroom chicken breast

If you have a large crowd coming over, increase this recipe and serve it in a chafing dish. I created it specifically for larger dinner parties because as it soaks up the sauce, the woodsy mushroom flavor with the hint of tangy balsamic just intensifies, so it's never a problem for it to sit out on a buffet.

Preheat the oven to 350 degrees F.

Combine the vegetable oil and 4 tablespoons of the butter in a large skillet over high heat. Once the butter and oil are bubbling, add the chicken breasts to the skillet four at a time. Sear on each side until the chicken is golden, about 2–3 minutes per side, then transfer them to a large baking dish. Repeat with the remaining breasts and set aside.

Melt the remaining 2 sticks of butter in the same skillet over medium heat. Add the onion and garlic and cook, stirring occasionally, until the onions are soft, 15 to 20 minutes. Add the mushrooms, stir, and raise the heat to high. Allow the mushrooms to cook until most of their liquid has evaporated, 15 to 20 minutes. Add the tomatoes and cook, shaking the pan, for 10 minutes, or until the tomatoes begin to break down. Add the vinegar, wine, salt, and pepper and bring to a boil. Reduce the heat and let simmer for 15 minutes.

Pour the mushroom mixture over the chicken and place the pan in the top half of the oven for 15 to 20 minutes, or until the chicken has just cooked through. Remove from the oven and serve each piece of chicken generously topped with mushroom mixture.

Yield: 8 servings
Preparation time: 30 minutes
Cooking time: 1 hour 15 minutes

3 tablespoons vegetable oil

1¼ cups unsalted butter
(2½ sticks)

8 boneless, skinless chicken
breasts, about 8 ounces each

6 cups sliced white mushrooms

1 large onion, thinly sliced

4 cloves garlic, chopped

2 pints cherry tomatoes,
quartered

6 tablespoons balsamic vinegar

2 cups Cabernet

2 teaspoons kosher salt

Freshly ground black pepper
to taste

MAKE AHEAD

Sauce can be made the day before.

French chicken Breast with orange Tarragon Butter

Pictured on page 2

Yield: 8 servings
Preparation time: 10 minutes
Cooking time: 30 minutes

¼ cup (½ stick) unsalted butter

¼ cup olive oil

8 "French" skin-on chicken breasts, 6–8 ounces each

Kosher salt and freshly ground black pepper

Fresh tarragon, for garnish

Orange Tarragon Butter, recipe follows

MAKE AHEAD

Chicken breasts must be made day of, but butter can be made up to 5 days in advance.

French chicken breasts have the first joint of the wing bone still attached so they're more elegant on the plate than boneless breasts. (You can ask your butcher to French them for you.) We try to use them as often as possible at large events because when you're plating dinner for 200 guests, you want a main course that will go from oven to plate quickly and beautifully.

Preheat the oven to 375 degrees F.

Warm 2 tablespoons of the butter and 2 tablespoons of the olive oil in a large skillet over high heat for 2 minutes. Season the chicken breasts with a sprinkling of salt and pepper.

Place four of the breasts in the pan skin side down. Sear for 2 to 3 minutes, or until the skin is crispy and golden brown. The skin will release from the pan when ready. Don't try to rush it—if you do you'll wind up leaving part of the skin stuck to the pan. Turn the breasts and sear for 1 more minute, then transfer them to a baking dish. Repeat the process with the rest of the butter, oil, and chicken.

Place the baking dish in the oven for 15 to 20 minutes. When the chicken is done, serve each piece with a slice of Orange Tarragon Butter, garnish with a sprig of tarragon, and serve immediately.

orange Tarragon Butter

½ cup (1 stick) unsalted butter, at room temperature

Zest of 1 orange

2 tablespoons orange juice

4 sprigs tarragon, leaves stripped and chopped

Pinch kosher salt

Mix the butter, orange zest, juice, tarragon, and salt. Place a 12-inch piece of plastic wrap on a flat surface and spoon the butter onto it, forming a log. Smooth the log out and roll it in the plastic wrap. Place in the refrigerator until ready to use. Cut slices on the bias to serve. Yield: 8 servings

grilled chicken, white bean, and basil chili

Steve is famous for planning last-minute dinners with friends that he usually lets me know about a couple of hours before the doorbell rings. This chili recipe is perfect for those unexpected informal get-togethers where you still want to eat well.

Place the grill pan over high heat until it begins to smoke, about 5 minutes. While the pan heats, toss the chicken with 1 teaspoon of the dried basil, a pinch of salt and pepper and 2 tablespoons of the olive oil. Place the chicken in the pan and grill for 3 to 4 minutes per side, or until the chicken is just cooked through. Remove from the pan and let cool 5 minutes. When cool enough to handle, cut into 1-inch chunks and set aside.

Pour the remaining olive oil into a heavy-bottomed pot and place over medium heat. Add the onion, garlic, and jalapeño and cook until translucent, about 10 minutes. Add the chicken, beans with their liquid, cumin, cinnamon, 1½ teaspoons salt, 1 teaspoon pepper, the remaining dried basil, the fresh basil, and the hot sauce.

Let the chili come to a slight boil, reduce the heat, and let it simmer for 20 minutes, stirring to make sure it doesn't stick. Serve in large mugs or bowls, topped with sour cream and garnished with a fresh basil leaf.

on the welcome wagon

I always say that I can see people get all squirrelly when they walk into a room and can't suss out where the bar is. And it's not just due to the calming effects of liquor; even the teetotalers are more comfortable once they have a prop in their hand. In fact, smokers will be the first to tell you that having something to do with your hands puts you more at ease. As a harried host, a simple "Welcome! The bar is over there—help yourself to something, and I'll be back to chat!" works every time.

Yield: 6–8 servings
Preparation time: 20 minutes
Cooking time: 40 minutes

2 pounds boneless, skinless chicken breast

1 tablespoon dried basil

Kosher salt

Freshly ground black pepper

¼ cup olive oil

1 Spanish onion, cut into ½-inch dice

1 large clove garlic, minced

1 small jalapeño, seeded and minced

Two 15-ounce cans great Northern beans

1½ tablespoons ground cumin

¼ teaspoon cinnamon

5 basil leaves, roughly chopped, plus additional leaves for garnish

1 tablespoon hot sauce such as Tabasco

Sour cream, for topping

SPECIAL EQUIPMENT

Cast-iron grill pan

MAKE AHEAD

Chili can be made the day before.

Duck sausage and white bean cassoulet

Yield: 8–10 servings
Preparation time: 30 minutes
Cooking time: 1½ hours

1 pound dried great Northern beans

1 pound duck sausage

1 small onion, whole

1 whole carrot

4 thyme sprigs

6 bay leaves

½ pound center-cut bacon, cut into 2-inch pieces

1 tablespoon olive oil

1 large onion, cut into 1-inch dice

2 large carrots, sliced into ¼-inch coins

10 cloves garlic, chopped

½ pound smoked kielbasa

1 cup Cabernet

14-ounce can low-sodium beef broth

¼ cup tomato paste

1 tablespoon kosher salt

2 teaspoons freshly ground black pepper

Crusty baguette, for serving

Cassoulet is a French peasant dish that was originally baked in a *cassole,* or earthenware pot. It sometimes contained duck or goose confit, often contained sausage, and always contained beans. My version is a bit of a hybrid—I do homage to the duck confit by using duck sausage, and although I cook mine on the stovetop, I still simmer the partially-cooked beans with the sausage mixture so they soak up that heady red wine sauce.

Preheat the oven to 375 degrees F.

Wash the beans well and put them in a large stockpot. Add enough water to the beans to cover by 2 inches and set over high heat. Bring to a boil for 2 minutes, remove from the heat, cover, and let stand 1 hour.

Put the duck sausage on a baking sheet and place it in the oven for 15 to 20 minutes. Remove and let cool. The sausage will not be fully cooked through.

Add the whole onion, whole carrot, two of the thyme sprigs, and three of the bay leaves to the beans. Add more water to the pot to cover again by 2 inches. Bring to a boil, lower the heat, and let simmer until the beans are mostly tender but with still a little bite to them, 50 to 60 minutes.

As the beans cook, put the bacon into a large skillet and place over medium heat. Cook until crispy and transfer the bacon to a paper towel–lined plate to

dinner napkins

I tend to feel guilty when I'm presented with an intricate origami napkin creation to unfold and make a mess of. I have always opted for something simpler and less affected. When we have guests at home, I especially like to use napkin rings. I pick them up on special or at garage sales and now have a few different types that I can choose from. Simply slipping a loose napkin through a ring is perfect for last-minute table settings, and I have to admit, I love having a prop to busy my hands with over coffee and conversation!

drain. Drain off all but about 1 tablespoon of the bacon fat from the skillet and add the olive oil. Return to the heat and add the diced onion, sliced carrots, and garlic and cook the mixture over low heat for 20 minutes, until the onion begins to turn translucent.

Slice both the duck sausage and the kielbasa on the bias into ½-inch-thick pieces and add them to the vegetable mix. Add the remaining bay leaves and thyme sprigs and cook, stirring, for 5 minutes. Next add the wine, broth, tomato paste, salt, and pepper. Raise the heat to high, bringing the mixture to a boil. Stir well to dissolve the tomato paste and lower the heat. Allow the mix to simmer for 5 minutes.

Remove the whole onion and carrot from the beans and add the vegetable and sausage mixture to the stockpot, leaving the pot on low heat. Stir well and cover. Let the cassoulet simmer for 15 to 20 minutes, or until most of the wine mixture has been absorbed by the beans. Spoon into a casserole dish and serve with crusty baguette on the side.

MAKE AHEAD

Cassoulet can be made the day before. To reheat, bring to room temperature and warm in a 350 degrees F oven for 30 minutes, stirring a couple of times as it warms.

pan-fried soft-shell crabs with chesapeake tartar sauce

Yield: 8 servings
Preparation Time: 20 minutes
Cooking Time: 10 minutes

16 soft-shell crabs, cleaned

6 cups buttermilk

About 2 cups canola oil

3 cups all-purpose flour

Kosher salt

Freshly ground black pepper

Chesapeake Tartar Sauce, recipe follows

Fresh mint leaves, for garnish

We were having dinner with a friend one night at HB, and at my suggestion, he ordered this dish. When it arrived at the table, he looked at it for a second, then asked the waiter for a crab cracker. I laughed, but when I realized he wasn't kidding, said, "Andrew, you eat the whole thing—that's the point of soft-shell crabs. They catch the crabs right after they've molted, before the new shell has had time to harden." He took a tentative first bite, the slightly crispy shell giving way to the sweet, tender flesh beneath, and got this big, goofy grin on his face. I can safely say that he'll be ordering soft-shells whenever they're in season from now on.

Place the soft-shell crabs in a nonreactive shallow baking dish and cover them with the buttermilk. Refrigerate for 10 minutes.

Pour the canola oil into a deep skillet, making sure there is enough to cover the crab entirely. (You may need more than 2 cups if your skillet is large.) Heat the oil until it reaches 350 degrees F on a deep-frying thermometer.

Combine the flour, 1 tablespoon salt, and 2 teaspoons pepper in a large bowl. Toss the crabs in the flour and place them carefully in the pan, leaving a couple of inches of space between them (which means you'll have to fry these in batches.). Be sure to step back as the crabs go in—the moisture in them will cause the oil to splatter. Fry the crabs until golden brown, 1 to 2 minutes. (Be sure not to overcook them. They'll be dry and tasteless if you do.) With a slotted spoon, remove the crabs from the pan and place on a paper towel. Transfer to a large oven safe platter and keep in a warm oven until all the crabs are cooked.

Lightly season the crabs to taste with additional salt and pepper. Place two crabs on each plate, top them with the Chesapeake tartar sauce, garnish with mint, and serve immediately.

chesapeake tartar sauce

½ cup good-quality mayonnaise, such as Hellmann's

1 tablespoon capers, roughly chopped

2 tablespoons Old Bay seasoning

1 tablespoon fresh lemon juice

Whisk all the ingredients together. Cover and chill. Yield: 1 cup

MAKE AHEAD

Crabs must be made just before serving, but tartar sauce can be made 5 days in advance.

ode to a dollar store

I have a love affair with Dollar Stores. If you're lucky enough to have one near you, think of it first when organizing your next shindig. I strongly recommend snooping around every now and then to pick up supplies—wineglasses, champagne glasses, ashtrays, disposable paper decorations, kitschy ornaments, *great* bargains on candles. You never know what treasures they'll have from week to week!

I once came across honey bear juice containers in a rainbow of super-sucrose colors. I repurposed them as outdoor tabletop decorations along with tall Hispanic religious candles. (Have you seen those? They're glass cylinder candles with pictures of saints. . . . They're colorful and pretty, and I love them. If you prefer, they're also available without the icon decal.)

As my mom says, "For a dollar, it doesn't owe you anything." So what if you never use them again?

seafood newburg with gremolata

Yield: 8–10 servings
Preparation Time: 30 minutes
Cooking Time: 45 minutes

½ cup all-purpose flour

2 tablespoons kosher salt

2 tablespoons paprika

1 teaspoon curry powder

¼ teaspoon ground nutmeg

¼ teaspoon cayenne

½ cup (1 stick) unsalted butter

2 shallots, minced

4 cups whole milk

¼ cup tomato paste

1 cup dry sherry

4 cups water

2 bay leaves

10 black peppercorns

1½ pounds sea scallops

1½ pounds large shrimp (16–20 count), peeled and deveined

1 pound lobster tail meat (2–3 tails), shell on

Steamed long-grain white rice, for serving

Gremolata, for garnish, recipe follows

As I've mentioned before, I like retro food—I really do. I suppose, in some way, it brings me back to my childhood—an era that I recently discovered has been labeled as "Mid-century." This Newburg recipe, updated by me, still has firm roots in my "Mid-century" upbringing. I can remember the first time I tasted the rich, tangy sauce with large chunks of seafood—it was a pretty swanky dish for a seven-year-old kid. It brings to mind an article in *The New Yorker* magazine. It commented on our fondness for things retro when it said, "Their meals seem like something someone's parents once ate, a campy *Joy of Cooking*." Well, alright then—I'll take that as a compliment.

To make the Newburg sauce, combine the flour, 1 tablespoon salt, paprika, curry powder, nutmeg, and cayenne in a small bowl and set aside. Melt the butter in a large saucepan over low heat. Add the shallots and cook, stirring, for 3 minutes, or until they begin to brown. While the shallots are cooking, bring the milk and tomato paste to a simmer in a saucepan over medium heat; be careful not to let it boil over. Add the flour mixture to the browned shallots and stir until mixed well with the butter. Add the sherry and whisk until smooth.

Add the hot milk mixture to the flour mixture slowly, whisking constantly until the mix is creamy and thick. Remove from heat and set aside.

Put 4 cups water, the bay leaves, the remaining salt and the peppercorns in another large saucepan and bring to a boil over high heat. Add the scallops and boil for 3 minutes. Using a slotted spoon, remove the scallops immediately and set them aside. Add the shrimp to the boiling water and repeat the same cooking process, then repeat it again with the lobster tails.

Once the lobster tails are cooked, remove them from the water and let them cool for a few minutes before extracting the meat from the shell. Chop it into large chunks.

Add the cooked shellfish to the Newburg sauce and bring to a simmer over low heat.

Serve over white rice, garnished with the gremolata.

gremolata

½ cup chopped flat-leaf parsley

2 tablespoons chopped fresh rosemary

2–3 cloves garlic, minced

2 tablespoons grated lemon zest

¼ teaspoon kosher salt

Mix all the ingredients together in a small bowl. Refrigerate until ready to use.

Yield: ¾ cup

crawfish étouffée

Long before I ever visited New Orleans, Cajun fare was one of my favorites. When Steve and I made it down there to celebrate the millennium, I just fell harder for the spicy, flavor-packed food. Étoufée is a particular favorite—this is my version. I like the veggies to still have a crunch and I like the crawfish to be plump and juicy. For those reasons this is a quick dish to prepare—perfect to serve when you're running late at work!

Heat the oil in a large skillet over high heat until it begins to smoke, 3 to 4 minutes. Add the flour all at once and whisk constantly until it turns a reddish-brown color, about 7 minutes.

Immediately lower the heat to medium and add the chopped vegetables and the seasoning mix. Keep stirring for about 5 minutes. Add the broth and stir until the mix thickens. Lower the heat and let the étoufée simmer for 15 minutes. Add the crawfish and simmer another 5 minutes. Remove from heat and serve over rice.

COOK'S NOTE: Use different colored peppers—red, yellow and green—if you can.

cajun seasoning mix

1 teaspoon kosher salt

1 teaspoon paprika

¾ teaspoon onion powder

½ teaspoon garlic powder

½ teaspoon dry mustard

¼ teaspoon freshly ground black pepper

¼ teaspoon cayenne

Mix all the ingredients in a small bowl and set aside.

Yield: 8 servings
Preparation time: 20 minutes
Cooking time: 30 minutes

3 tablespoons vegetable oil

¼ cup all-purpose flour

1 medium onion cut into 1-inch dice

1 large celery rib cut into 1-inch dice

2 large bell peppers cut into 1-inch dice, see note

Cajun Seasoning Mix, recipe follows

2 cups low-sodium vegetable broth

1 pound crawfish tail meat, peeled

Steamed long-grain white rice, for serving

MAKE AHEAD

Étoufée is best made day of, but can be made the day before and reheated.

salmon wellington

Yield: 8–10 servings
Preparation time: 35 minutes
Cooking time: 40 minutes

3 leeks

6 tablespoons unsalted butter

1 red onion, thinly sliced

2 tablespoons dried tarragon

½ cup Chardonnay

1 teaspoon kosher salt

1 teaspoon freshly ground
black pepper

2 puff pastry sheets, thawed

Flour, for the work surface

1 egg, beaten with 2 tea-
spoons water

3-pound salmon fillet, skin
removed

Dijon Whipped Cream, recipe
follows

This has been one of our party staples for years. We think it's so good, we managed to make it on *The Next Food Network Star* and again on *Party Line.* The presentation wows guests every time!

Preheat the oven to 350 degrees F.

Trim the leeks, making sure to only use the tender white and pale green part. Split them in half lengthwise and clean well under running water to remove all dirt. Cut into thin slices and set aside.

Melt the butter in a large skillet over medium heat. Add the leeks, onion, and tarragon and cook until the onion mix is soft, about 10 minutes. Add the wine, raise the heat to high, and bring to a boil. Let the liquid cook off, add the salt and pepper, remove from heat, and set aside to cool for 10 minutes.

Unfold one pastry sheet and lay it on a lightly floured surface. Brush one edge with the egg wash and overlap the other sheet by 2 inches. Roll the pastry out until it's big enough to enclose the whole piece of salmon.

Spoon the cooled onion mixture down the center of the pastry, place the salmon on top of that, and fold the pastry over all. Brush the edges with more egg wash and press well to seal them.

ready, set...

You know what bugs me? When I arrive at a party, and the host isn't dressed and showered. That is a sure way to get your party off to a rocky start—it makes the guests feel awkward and sets a frantic tone before the evening begins. Be sure you're put together and have your face on, then early birds can keep you company in the kitchen as you finish your last-minute preparations. Not being ready with all your food and drinks happens to the best of us and is easily forgiven. Leaving guests to fend for themselves while you shower . . . not so much.

Place the salmon parcel seam side down on a sheet pan. Brush it with egg wash and place it in the oven for 30 to 40 minutes, until the pastry is puffed and golden brown. Let the salmon sit for 15 minutes before slicing. Serve with Dijon Whipped Cream on the side.

dijon whipped cream

1 cup heavy cream

1 tablespoon Dijon mustard

1 teaspoon kosher salt

½ teaspoon white pepper

SPECIAL EQUIPMENT:
Chilled stainless-steel bowl

Pour the cream into the bowl and whisk until soft peaks begin to form. Add the mustard, salt, and pepper and continue to whisk until stiff peaks form. Refrigerate until ready to use. Yield: 1½–2 cups

Baked Rotini with Tomato Cream

Yield: 8–10 servings.
Preparation time: 30 minutes
Cooking time: 30 minutes

½ cup olive oil
6 cloves garlic, minced

1 large onion, diced

3 zucchini, sliced lengthwise
and cut into ½-inch pieces

4 carrots, sliced lengthwise and
cut into ¼-inch pieces

2 teaspoons dried basil

Kosher salt and freshly ground
black pepper to taste

2 packed cups baby spinach

28-ounce can crushed tomatoes

2 cups heavy cream

2 pounds rotini pasta

2 pounds fontina cheese,
shredded

½ cup fresh basil, chopped

1 cup shredded Parmesan

This is a sinfully easy and delicious recipe, great for a quick family meal or feeding a large number of guests at a buffet. The Fontina cheese gives it a distinctive, creamy taste, and the fresh veggies help make it a one-dish dinner.

Preheat the oven to 350 degrees F.

Warm the oil in a deep skillet over high heat. Add the garlic and onion and cook until the garlic begins to turn golden. Add the zucchinis, carrots, dried basil, and salt and pepper, lower the heat to medium, and cook until the vegetables are mostly tender but with still a little firmness, 10 to 12 minutes.

Add the spinach and cook until wilted. Stir in the crushed tomatoes and heavy cream and let simmer for 10 minutes.

Fill a large pot three quarters full with water and place it over high heat. Bring to a boil, add plenty of salt (it should taste like the sea), and add the rotini. Stir and let cook until al dente, about 9 minutes. Drain the pasta well and pour it back into the pot.

Add the vegetable and sauce mixture, 4 cups of the fontina, and the fresh basil to the cooked pasta. Mix well and spoon into a large oven-safe casserole dish. Top with the remaining fontina and Parmesan and bake the casserole in the top half of the oven for 15 minutes. Remove and serve immediately.

it doesn't make scents

Dan's mom has a thing about scented candles. Well, actually, she has a thing about scented everything (as well as those little plush animals that sing when you press their feet, but that's off the subject.) She's a terrific cook, but I can never understand why she'd allow a cranberry-scented candle to compete with the aroma of her Braciola. This is a hard and fast rule for me at events: Always use non-scented candles on the tables so that guests can smell the fruits (or Braciola) of your labor.

three-cheese spaghetti pie

My dad likes to say that my mother cooks for an army, and I'll admit that I inherited the trait. I live in fear of running out of food, so I'm always cooking way more than is needed. The upside of that is that we always have leftovers in our fridge—something I happen to love!

One day I found some leftover spaghetti in the refrigerator, tossed it in a bowl with some other odds and ends, added egg and cream, and put the whole thing in a skillet. It was one of the best quick meals we'd ever had.

Preheat oven to 350 degrees F.

Bring a large pot of water to a boil. Salt generously and add the spaghetti. Bring back to a boil and cook for 11 to 13 minutes until the spaghetti is al dente. Drain into a colander and rinse under cold water. Return the spaghetti to the pot and set aside.

Heat 2 tablespoons of the olive oil in a medium-sized skillet over medium heat for 1 minute. Add the garlic and onion and cook for 3 minutes, stirring occasionally. Add the tomatoes, olives, 1 teaspoon of the salt, and a few grinds of pepper and cook for an additional 5 minutes, until the tomatoes begin to break down. You can help the process along by crushing them with the back of a spoon as they get soft.

Remove the mixture from the heat and set aside.

Whisk the eggs and cream together in a large mixing bowl. Add the remaining teaspoon of salt, pepper to taste, the red pepper flakes, chopped basil, fontina, feta, 4 ounces of the Parmesan, and the tomato mixture. Mix in the spaghetti.

Heat the remaining olive oil in the skillet over high heat. Add the spaghetti mixture, reduce the heat to medium, and cook for 5 minutes. Place the skillet in the oven for 30 minutes, until the center of the pie is set and the top is golden.

Remove the pie from the oven and let cool for 10 minutes. Run a spatula around the edges and underneath the pie to loosen it, then invert the pie onto a large plate. Place another plate onto the pie and flip it again so the browned side is up. Let set for an additional 10 minutes.

Slice the pie, garnishing each serving with a sprinkle of the remaining Parmesan and the whole basil leaves.

Yield: 6–8 servings
Preparation Time: 20 minutes
Cooking Time: 1 hour

¾ pound spaghetti

6 tablespoons olive oil

5 cloves garlic, coarsely chopped

1 small onion, thinly sliced

16 cherry tomatoes, halved

16 kalamata olives, pitted and halved

2 teaspoons kosher salt

Freshly ground black pepper

4 eggs

1 cup heavy cream

1 teaspoon crushed red pepper (optional)

6 fresh basil leaves, chopped, plus additional whole leaves for garnish

4 ounces Fontina cheese, shredded

8 ounces feta, crumbled

8 ounces Parmesan, shredded

SPECIAL EQUIPMENT

10-inch oven-safe cast-iron or nonstick skillet

MAKE AHEAD

Pie can be prepared the day before and reheated.

sweet pea, tarragon, and chèvre frittata

My grandfather was one of those Italians from the old country who thought of cooking as women's work. Consequently, he left the job to my grandmother, who was a fabulous cook. When she passed on, my mother, being his only daughter, was left to do the cooking for him. The one thing he could cook, though, was eggs.

Every once in a great while, when my parents would go out, and he'd wind up watching me, he'd haul out the big cast-iron skillet, put plenty of olive oil in it, and proceed to make delicious open-faced omelets. He filled them with fresh vegetables from his garden, pungent cheeses, and occasionally homemade sausages. They were light, fluffy, and slightly golden on top. We'd sit at the kitchen table and eat the whole thing—it was a secret we kept between us— I think he was afraid he'd have to cook more often if my mother found out!.

Preheat the oven to 350 degrees F.

Warm the olive oil in the skillet over medium-high heat for 1 minute. Meanwhile, whisk the eggs together in a large mixing bowl with the salt, pepper, and tarragon.

Pour the egg mixture into the preheated pan. After 30 seconds, use a spatula to pull the sides of the frittata away from the pan and allow the uncooked egg mixture to flow over the sides and underneath the cooked portion.

Add the peas and goat cheese and place the skillet in the top half of the oven for 14 minutes, or until the center of the frittata is set. Remove the skillet from the oven and let cool for 10 minutes. Run the spatula around the sides of the skillet to loosen the frittata and shake gently to see if the bottom is free. If not, gently loosen it with the spatula. Slide the frittata onto a decorative plate and slice it into wedges. Serve warm or at room temperature.

Yield: 8 wedges
Preparation time: 10 minutes
Cooking time: 15 minutes

3 tablespoons olive oil

8 eggs

1½ teaspoons kosher salt

½ teaspoon freshly ground black pepper

2 tablespoons dried tarragon

½ cup frozen peas, thawed

½ cup goat cheese, crumbled

SPECIAL EQUIPMENT

10-inch oven-safe cast-iron or nonstick skillet

side dishes

Before I was a caterer, my family tried an ambitious thing. We threw my little sister, Jackie, her wedding reception. The idea was carefully planned out. The ceremony would take place in a tiny chapel near Mom's home in Rhode Island and would be followed by a bayside reception at a storybook perfect New England bed-and-breakfast. It was all meant to be very Gatsby. The rolling lawns had a sparkling view of the bay. We'd rent white tents and cloths, serve chilled salmon, cold sides, family favorites, and wine.

In retrospect, it was great fun as we all chipped in. Family flew in from England laden with beautiful Stiltons and Cheddars. Mom and a friend drove out to Michigan for a fishing expedition and came home with two gigantic salmon. You'll think I'm embellishing if I tell you that she contacted a local celebrity chef, who was so intrigued by the story that he cooked those salmon on his TV show, but it's true. Then Mom and my aunts got to work on the side dishes. For two days the sisters sequestered themselves in the vast kitchen of this grand old house. Fresh rosemary was snipped from Mom's garden and added to Israeli couscous with dried figs, colorful nasturtiums were plucked and tossed with wild greens and a shallot vinaigrette, tender new potatoes became a cold salad with tarragon and crumbled Stilton. Rentals were ordered, staff was reserved, jam tarts and fruit trifles were prepared. Everything was flawlessly assembled for our feast of smuggled cheeses and celebrity salmon.

The big day came, and my predawn memory is a friend of Mom's rustling Jackie out of bed. He was showing her this stunning eight-foot bower of fresh hydrangea, panicked that it wasn't on his floral to-do list. Jackie knew all the flower arrangements for the wedding but didn't recognize this one. Rubbing her eyes and mumbling that she was pretty sure that this wedding arch was meant to be a surprise, she packed the bower into her van and headed off to the church for setup.

From that point on things got pretty crazed. I remember standing in the dewy grass among piles of rentals wondering how in the world to set up the

tents; our friend, Tony, running last-minute errands with the keys to the car that was meant to transport my sister to the church; poor Mom rushing to complete the buffet displays and getting to the church only moments before Jackie made her entrance; and lastly, the bride herself, having just finished running around town with a staple gun, hanging "This Way to the Church" signs on telephone poles, walking down the aisle with her hair still wet from the shower.

I use this story as an example of why it's good to hire professionals to help you out. I also use it as an example that although things do sometimes go wrong at your perfect event, you will always remember the good stuff: Jackie, looking fabulous in her hand-sewn dress, laughing as she makes her way across the green grass against the backdrop of a brilliant blue ocean; the sisters posing proudly behind the buffet of gorgeous foods they'd lovingly prepared. But most clearly, I remember wondering, when the hell did Mom become a fisherman?

oven-roasted yukon gold potatoes

Yield: 8 servings
Preparation time: 15 minutes
Cooking time: 30 minutes

3 pounds Yukon gold potatoes, washed and cut into wedges

¼ cup olive oil

2 teaspoons kosher salt

1 teaspoon freshly ground black pepper

2 cloves garlic, minced

1 sprig fresh thyme, leaves picked

1 sprig fresh rosemary leaves stripped

1 tablespoon chopped fresh parsley

Yukon golds are best known for their color and buttery-tasting flesh. They're perfect for roasting. I think this is a great "go-to" recipe, since it's a side dish that pairs well with beef, pork, chicken, and fish. We sometimes serve these as a bed for meat, like rice. The juices mingle with the crispy potatoes in a really delicious way.

Preheat the oven to 400 degrees F.

In a large bowl, toss the potatoes with the oil, salt, pepper, garlic, thyme and rosemary leaves and parsley. Spread the potatoes on a baking sheet and roast them in the top half of the oven for 40 to 50 minutes, or until the potatoes are fork-tender, golden brown, and crispy. Serve immediately.

truffled mashed potatoes

Truffles sell anywhere from $100 to $300 per pound. That's a perfect reason to use truffle oil—it imparts the pungent, earthy taste that truffles are famous for at a fraction of the cost. These potatoes would stand up perfectly at the fanciest dinner party, but I've got to say, they make a great comfort food too. Sometimes when Steve isn't home, I'll make some for myself and just eat them in my sweats in front of the TV.

Put the potatoes into a large saucepan and cover with water. Place over high heat and bring to a boil. Cook until fork-tender, about 25 minutes. Drain the potatoes and return them to low heat for 2 to 3 minutes to get rid of excess water.

Warm the cream and butter in a small saucepan over medium heat until the butter melts.

Using a masher, mash the potatoes right in the saucepan. Add the garlic, cream-and-butter mixture, salt, and pepper and mix well using a large spoon. Stir in the truffle oil and serve.

Yield: 8 servings
Preparation time: 15 minutes
Cooking time: 25 minutes

3 pounds Russet potatoes, peeled and cut into 2-inch dice

1½ cups light cream

6 tablespoons unsalted butter

2 cloves garlic, minced

2½ teaspoons kosher salt

1 teaspoon freshly ground black pepper

2 tablespoons black truffle oil

tater mountain

Scotty was a server in our gourmet takeaway who once helped out by smoothing the mashed potatoes into a solid, white, potato snowball. I had to explain that smooth and shiny food can indeed be tempting; chocolate ganache, M&Ms and Ring Dings come to mind; but that a glossy dome of mashed potatoes maybe doesn't fall into the same category.

Always keep texture in mind when presenting your meals. Food just looks more appealing when it is allowed its own natural movement. I'm not saying be messy, though, so remember that when you're serving from large bowls and platters, keep the sides neat and wiped clean of spills.

fingerling potato hash

Yield: 8 servings
Preparation time: 10 minutes
Cooking time: 30 minutes

3 tablespoons unsalted butter

3 tablespoons olive oil

2 large shallots, thinly sliced

3 pounds fingerling potatoes, sliced ⅛ inch thick (see note)

1 tablespoon kosher salt

Freshly ground black pepper

A fingerling potato is the shape of—what else?—a stubby finger. I love the presentation they make sliced on a dinner plate—the little round coins are just fun to look at! But because of their size, it's a lot of work to prepare them for a crowd. My suggestion is to save this dish for intimate dinner parties.

Melt the butter and olive oil in a large skillet over medium heat. Add the shallots and cook until they begin to soften, about 3 minutes. Add the potatoes, raise the heat a bit, and toss to coat. Cook, stirring occasionally, until the potatoes are brown and crispy, 20 to 30 minutes. Remove from the heat and serve.

COOK'S NOTE: Substitute red or Yukon potatoes if you can't find fingerlings—but try to find them!

centerpieces

Large centerpieces can inhibit conversation. I'm sure you've been to a wedding where the bride artfully placed a floral monsterpiece that completely blocked your view of the guests sitting across from you. Keep your centerpieces low and tasteful, especially when hosting dinner parties in your home. Rather than large candelabras or tall vases that give the table visual height, think about emphasizing the table's length. Employ a length of leafy greens, branches, or boughs dotted with tealight votives. We love the impact of an eclectic grouping of low candleholders in assorted finishes and shapes. You can achieve a similar effect with small pots of fresh herbs, a composition of holiday ornaments, or other collections of miniature items.

old Bay and Lemon Roasted potatoes

Whenever we make these potatoes in the catering kitchen, we have to put a sign on them as they sit on the cooling racks—"Do not touch!" I'm probably the reason for the sign. I can't stop myself from picking at them as I pass by. One here, one there, until the supply starts to dwindle. It's the combination of the tart lemon juice and slightly spicy, pungent Old Bay seasoning mix that makes them irresistible.

Preheat the oven to 400 degrees F.

Put the potatoes into a large mixing bowl and add the olive oil, Old Bay, salt, lemon zest, lemon juice and the lemon slices. Toss well and spread the mixture on a baking sheet, making sure the potato cubes lie flat.

Roast the potatoes for 45 to 55 minutes, turning them with a metal spatula at least once. When done, the potatoes will be crisp and golden on the outside and fork-tender on the inside. Remove from the oven and serve immediately.

Yield: 8 servings
Preparation time: 20 minutes
Cooking time: 55 minutes

3 pounds red potatoes, cut into 1½-inch dice

½ cup olive oil

1½ tablespoons Old Bay seasoning

1 teaspoon kosher salt

2 tablespoons lemon zest

½ cup fresh lemon juice

1 lemon, sliced and pitted

beautify the bath

Don't forget that your guests will be using your bathroom, so make sure it's up to par as well. Personal belongings should be removed from the sink and counters—this includes the bar of soap and towels that your family uses daily. You don't need to go crazy with mini seashell-shaped soaps and embroidered hand towels, but a few touches will be remembered. It's nice to provide a liquid soap and thick paper guest towels; a more sanitary option for your guests. And no one likes to go from a subtly lit room to the glaring overheads of the bath, so a candle or two is always a good idea. For safety reasons, just be sure to use enclosed votives that can be left unattended.

herbed porridge

Yield: 8–10 servings
Preparation time: 10 minutes
Cooking time: 30 minutes

½ cup (1 stick) unsalted butter

1¾ cups grits

½ cup long-grain white rice

¼ cup wheat germ

4 thyme sprigs

8 fresh sage leaves, chopped

1 bunch chives, chopped

2 sprigs tarragon, leaves
stripped and chopped

1 tablespoon kosher salt

¾ teaspoon freshly ground
black pepper

For most of us, porridge is just something that Goldilocks ate. But who actually ever really knew what it was? Well, I'm here to tell you that it's a mix of grains that, by themselves can be pretty bland but with the addition of rich, creamy butter and savory herbs are made irresistible. They make a perfect bed for the French Chicken Breast with Orange Tarragon Butter (page 110).

Put 6½ cups water in a large saucepan with the butter and bring to a boil over high heat. Add the grits, rice, and wheat germ and stir well. Lower the heat to medium and add the thyme, sage, chives, tarragon, salt, and pepper. Cook, stirring often, until the water has been absorbed, 20 to 30 minutes. It will have an oatmeal-like consistency. Remove the thyme sprigs and serve immediately.

saffron Risotto cakes

Risotto cakes are another wonderfully unexpected side dish. The saffron, which is the dried stigma of a type of crocus, turns the risotto a vibrant yellow, and the flavor is delicate yet pervasive. These complement both chicken and fish and are worth the time it takes to make them.

Pour the chicken broth into a saucepan and bring it to a simmer over medium heat.

Put the butter and olive oil in a second saucepan and melt over medium heat. Add the shallot and garlic to the oil, lower the heat, and cook for 10 minutes or until translucent. Add the rice, saffron and salt and stir for 5 minutes, until the rice begins to turn translucent. Add the warmed wine and stir until all of it has been absorbed. Begin to add the chicken broth ½ cup at a time. After each addition, stir until most of the liquid has been absorbed, but add more broth before the rice begins to stick. Continue until all of the broth has been used. The risotto will have a creamy texture, but the grains will still be a bit al dente.

Pour the mixture onto a baking sheet and allow it to cool completely before continuing.

When the risotto has cooled, scoop it into a mixing bowl, mix in the 2 eggs, and form the risotto into cakes roughly 1 inch high and 3 inches in diameter, making sure to compress the cakes so they don't fall apart.

Pour ½ inch of vegetable oil into a skillet and heat for 2 minutes over a medium-high heat. Gently place the cakes in the pan four at a time and fry on both sides until golden, 2 to 3 minutes per side. Using a slotted spoon, transfer them to a baking sheet and keep them warm in a 200-degree oven until all the cakes have been fried. Serve warm.

Yield: 8–10 cakes
Preparation time: 15 minutes
Cooking time: 40 minutes

4 cups low-sodium chicken broth

3 tablespoons unsalted butter

2 tablespoons olive oil

2 tablespoons minced shallot

1 clove garlic, minced

2 cups Arborio rice

½ teaspoon saffron threads

1 teaspoons kosher salt

1 cup Sauvignon Blanc, warmed

2 eggs

Vegetable oil

MAKE AHEAD

Risotto can be made the day before. Cakes should be fried day of.

tarragon and sweet pea puree

Yield: 4 cups
Preparation time: 5 minutes

Two 32-ounce packages frozen peas

2 tablespoons dried tarragon

½ teaspoon kosher salt

1 teaspoon white pepper

1 cup heavy cream

Growing up, my brother, Jim, hated peas—still does to this day. I remember dinner table battles where he steadfastly refused to eat them, no matter what the consequence. Amazingly, at a holiday dinner I prepared, he tried this creamy, slightly sweet puree and actually liked it. I can't think of a better recommendation.

Put the peas into a saucepan and cover with water. Place over high heat and bring to a boil. Cook 1 minute, remove from the heat, and drain. Put the peas into a blender, add the tarragon, salt, pepper, and cream and blend until smooth, about 20 seconds. Serve immediately.

fig and rosemary couscous

Yield: 8 cups
Preparation time: 15 minutes
Cooking time: 20 minutes

6 tablespoons olive oil

Leaves of 6 rosemary sprigs

4 cups Israeli couscous

8 cups chicken stock

1 tablespoon Dijon mustard

2 cups dried Mission figs, stems trimmed, quartered

2 teaspoons ground cardamom

2 teaspoons kosher salt

1 teaspoon freshly ground black pepper

The Israeli couscous used in this recipe is larger than the more commonly known Moroccan couscous and, for my money, has a more luxurious texture. Sometimes called pearl couscous, it's only become widely available in the U.S. in the past ten years. The grains—made from semolina wheat—are pea-sized and can be cooked like rice.

Warm the olive oil and rosemary in a large, heavy-bottomed saucepan over high heat. When the rosemary begins to sizzle, about 1 minute, add the couscous. Stir to coat well and cook for 2 minutes, stirring frequently. Add the chicken stock, mustard, figs, cardamom, salt, and pepper, lower the heat, and let simmer until all the stock has been absorbed, about 20 minutes. Remove from the heat, fluff with a fork, and serve immediately.

mahogany rice pilaf

I have to say, rice pilaf usually leaves me feeling cold, but a lot of clients request it. Rather than just make the standard version, I found a deep reddish-brown rice that, when cooked, keeps a chewy texture and slightly nutty flavor. Combined with dried fruits and brandy, it makes a rice pilaf that's both striking and—if I do say so myself—delicious.

Warm the oil in a large, deep skillet over medium heat for 2 to 3 minutes. Add the onion and cook, stirring, until slightly translucent, 3 to 4 minutes. Add the rice and stir well to coat. Next add the Calvados and stir. Cook for 2 to 3 minutes. Add the broth and salt, bring to a boil, and reduce to a simmer. Cover the skillet and cook until most of the liquid has soaked into the rice, about 35 minutes.

Add half of the chopped fruit and continue to cook until all of the liquid has been absorbed. Remove from the heat and stir in the remainder of the fruit, along with the chopped green onion and parsley. Serve immediately.

COOK'S NOTE: Lundberg makes a great mahogany rice blend that can be found in specialty stores such as Whole Foods or health food stores. Use a mixture of dried fruits such as apples, apricots, raisins, cranberries, figs and plums.

Yield: 8 servings
Preparation time: 10 minutes
Cooking time: 45 minutes

¼ cup vegetable oil
½ large onion, diced
2 cups mahogany rice (see note)
¼ cup Calvados
4 cups low-sodium vegetable broth
1 tablespoon kosher salt
1 cup mixed dried fruit, roughly chopped (see note)
¼ cup chopped green onions
¼ cup chopped flat-leaf parsley

meal ticket

When calculating how much food to prepare, always take into account the hour of your party. Specifically, if you're inviting guests after work, be aware that they'll expect a meal. Even if you haven't prepared a meal, and have told them this isn't going to be a meal, and they've told you they understand it's not a meal, know that your hungry guests will make a meal out of whatever is there. Learn from my experience—make extra!

pearl barley tabbouleh

Yield: 8 servings
Preparation time: 15 minutes
Cooking time: 40 minutes

3 teaspoons kosher salt

¾ cup pearl barley

¼ cup extra-virgin olive oil

3 tablespoons fresh lemon juice

4 cups plum tomatoes, diced
(10-12 tomatoes)

1 cup chopped fresh parsley

3 tablespoons chopped fresh
basil

2 tablespoons chopped fresh
rosemary

MAKE AHEAD

Tabbouleh can be made
the day before.

Tabbouleh is traditionally prepared with bulghur wheat and eaten as part of a mezze (a selection of Middle Eastern appetizers). I thought it would be fun to switch the bulghur to pearl barley, which makes this a heartier side dish. It's perfect for a summer meal. The importance of using the freshest ingredients in this dish can't be stressed enough.

Bring 4 cups water to a boil in a large saucepan over high heat. Add 2 teaspoons of the salt and the barley. Stir, reduce the heat to medium, and cook until the barley is tender, about 40 minutes.

Drain the barley, rinse it under cold water, drain again, and place it in a large mixing bowl. Add the remaining salt, the olive oil, lemon juice, tomatoes, and herbs and toss. Refrigerate for at least 2 hours.

pick me!

It seems that everybody's holiday get-together is scheduled for the same night. As you desperately hope people will choose you and your party, you're reminded of being picked last at junior high school volleyball games.

This is just one of the times that open houses are a great option. First off, there's something old school and Currier and Ives about them, which I just love. Plus, they're often afternoon parties, which is such a nice change during a busy social season.

But no matter what time of year you're having your open house, you run the risk of having all your guests turn up at the opening bell. Easy fix? Stagger the times on your invitations. For example, if your party is from 1 to 6 P.M., invite half the guests from 1 to 4 P.M. and the other half from 3 to 6 P.M.

And don't forget the best reason to throw an open house: You have an end time listed, which allows you to make plans for later that day (and pick whose parties *you* choose to go to).

caraway Roasted Brussels sprouts

Yield: 8 servings
Preparation time: 15 minutes
Cooking time: 30 minutes

2 pounds Brussels sprouts, trimmed and halved

⅔ cup olive oil

2 teaspoons caraway seeds

2 teaspoons kosher salt

MAKE AHEAD

Brussels sprouts can be made the day before and reheated in a 350 degree F oven for 15–20 minutes.

Steve grew up eating boiled, mushy Brussels sprouts, which he still loves. I grew up avoiding them because I didn't like the texture or the cabbage-like flavor. But when I was in my early 20s I went to dinner at a friend's house, and she roasted them—and I loved them! I've been roasting them ever since. They're crunchy on the outside, tender on the inside, and have a slightly nutty flavor. The caraway is a great complement and you'll wind up fighting over the crunchy, dark brown outer leaves—we do!

Preheat the oven to 375 degrees F.

Toss all the ingredients together in a large mixing bowl. Spread the Brussels sprouts out on a baking sheet large enough to hold them in one layer and place them in the top half of the oven. Roast until the sprouts are fork-tender and nicely browned, 25 to 30 minutes. Some of the leaves of the sprouts will break off during the roasting process and get dark brown. Mix them with the sprouts before serving—they add a great flavor. Serve hot.

dim some

I should get a kickback from hardware stores because I am the spokesperson for dimmer switches. I am such a fan of low light that when you come to our house for dinner you need a miner's helmet to find the bar. Dimmer switches, candles, and tabletop lamps are the only way to light an evening affair. Think of how an intimate restaurant is lit, as opposed to a diner, and how the lighting affects not only the room's atmosphere but the look of the food. Bring the lights down and keep in mind that subtle shadows add an appealing sense of romance.

Braised Leeks with sel de mer

Leeks aren't too often thought of as a stand-alone side dish, but their subtle, slightly sweet, oniony flavor works really well with chicken and beef. Two bonuses to this dish: It's easy to make, and it will surprise your guests.

Preheat the oven to 350 degrees F.

The white and pale green section of the leek is the most tender, so trim away the dark green, tough end and slice off the root end. Slice the leeks lengthwise and rinse well under cold water, making sure to get between all the leaves.

Place the leeks in a baking dish and pour the wine over them. Dot them with butter and sprinkle with sel de mer and pepper. Bake, uncovered, for 30 to 40 minutes, until they are fork-tender. Remove from the braising liquid and serve immediately.

Yield: 8 servings
Preparation time: 10 minutes
Cooking time: 40 minutes

4 large leeks

2 cups Chardonnay

3 tablespoons unsalted butter, cut into bits

1 tablespoon sel de mer (sea salt)

2 teaspoons freshly ground black pepper

Anise Roasted Green Beans

The anise seed really makes this recipe special. The slight licorice flavor has a surprising punch. Plus, roasting the green beans until they begin to shrivel gives them an interesting texture—soft in the center and crunchy on the ends.

Preheat the oven to 375 degrees F.

Toss all the ingredients together in a large mixing bowl and arrange them in one layer on two baking sheets. Roast the beans until they begin to shrivel, 20 to 30 minutes. Serve immediately.

Yield: 8–10 servings
Preparation time: 5 minutes
Cooking time: 30 minutes

3 pounds green beans, trimmed

½ cup olive oil

1 tablespoon anise seeds

2 teaspoons kosher salt

pan-sautéed vegetable confetti

Yield: 8 servings
Preparation time: 10 minutes
Cooking time: 6 minutes

4 medium carrots cut into ½-inch dice

3 medium zucchini cut into ½-inch dice

3 summer squash cut into ½-inch dice

1 large red bell pepper cut into ½-inch dice

1 cup frozen, shelled edamame (soy beans)

¼ cup olive oil

2 teaspoons kosher salt

½ teaspoon freshly ground black pepper

½ cup thinly sliced green onions

MAKE AHEAD

Confetti can be made the day before.

We work out of a lot of alternative spaces in Chicago—meaning art galleries, museums, fashion houses—and the one thing all have in common is a lack of kitchens. That leaves us with the challenge of coming up with dishes that travel and reheat well. That's why I came up with this recipe—it's all of those things, plus rustically beautiful and delicious. It's one of our most requested dishes at wedding dinners.

Mix the carrots, zucchini, squash, bell pepper, and edamame together in a large bowl and set aside.

Warm the oil in a large skillet over high heat for 2 minutes. Add the vegetables, along with the salt and pepper. Sauté for 5 minutes, or until the vegetables are slightly tender—the carrots will still have a crunch to them, and that's okay. Add the green onions and sauté for 1 more minute. Serve immediately.

inspired sides

Even a simple grilled menu can be bumped up by making unexpected choices. Our friends Matt and Regan had a beachside wedding and threw themselves a low-key barbecue afterward. They could have gone with a basic menu, but it was, after all, a wedding celebration. Instead of burgers, brats, and beer, they opted to serve buffalo burgers, wild boar and venison sausages, and a wonderful assortment of hard-to-find microbrews. They replaced old condiment standbys with wasabi mustard, heirloom tomatoes, and grilled brioche buns.

I think this is a great tip for any home chef: Whether it's tossing anise into fresh green beans or truffle oil into mashed potatoes, little twists can turn a simple dish into an inspired one. In fact, we were so impressed with the grilled feast that we allowed Regan an hour's reprieve from our harassment. We had been giggling from the moment the pastor rechristened her Mrs. Regan Fagan.

oven-roasted root vegetables

These are the perfect accompaniment to the Cider Braised Pork Loin (see page 99), and even though I'm a confirmed summer person, I always look forward to autumn so that I can roast a batch of these.

Preheat the oven to 375 degrees F.

Toss all the ingredients together in a large mixing bowl. Divide the vegetables between two baking sheets and roast until the vegetables are fork-tender and browned, 35 to 45 minutes. Serve immediately.

off the carts

First the bad news. Placing a vase of supermarket flowers in the center of a table does not make you Martha. But the supermarket flower prices can be great and the good news is that even the ugliest arrangement can still be used in attractive ways!

Take these arrangements apart and use the flowers separately to accent your table. After trimming them short, hide the flower's stems under dishes and between the folds of the cloth so that only the blossoms are peeking out and filling in the blank areas with color. You can also pull the petals off and sprinkle them down the center of the table—this is a good trick when you want to use roses that are about to wilt. When I have leftover flowers I cut them very short and place groupings in small tumblers or mini vases. I use these to give a little punch in areas like the bathroom or hallway. Lastly, after careful thought and consideration, I take all the baby's breath and throw it away.

Although flowers are always good for a buffet, I find that greens are even better and add an intriguing sophistication. I love the textural look of clipped ivy trailing down from a riser, delicate bayberry leaves around a cheese display, and soft pines dressing up a holiday table.

Yield: 8–10 servings
Preparation time: 20 minutes
Cooking time: 45 minutes

2 large parsnips, peeled and cut on the bias into 2-inch pieces

2 large carrots, peeled and cut on the bias into 2-inch pieces

4 medium-size turnips, cut into 2-inch chunks

1 large celery root, trimmed and cut into 2-inch chunks

4 medium-size beets, peeled and cut into 2-inch chunks

4 medium shallots, peeled and quartered

½ cup olive oil

3 teaspoons kosher salt

2 teaspoons freshly ground black pepper

Leaves from 4 sprigs fresh thyme

cauliflower cheddar gratin

Yield: 8 servings
Preparation time: 35 minutes
Cooking time: 30 minutes

Kosher salt

2 heads cauliflower, cut into florets

½ cup (1 stick) unsalted butter, plus additional for the baking dish

2 bay leaves

Leaves from 1 sprig thyme

¼ cup all-purpose flour

2 cloves garlic, minced

3 tablespoons dry vermouth

3 cups whole milk, scalded

24 ounces sharp Cheddar, grated (about 3 cups)

4 ounces Gruyère (about ½ cup)

1 teaspoon white pepper

1 cup seasoned bread crumbs

1 tablespoon chopped fresh parsley

Steve's a big fan of cauliflower with cheese sauce. He had it growing up—it was the quintessential early-'70s vegetable dish. The authentic version is boiled cauliflower with Velveeta or, God help us, canned Cheddar cheese soup, but I took the idea and dressed it up a little. It makes a great side dish for larger dinner parties.

Preheat the oven to 400 degrees F.

Fill a large pot halfway with water and bring it to a boil over high heat. Salt the water liberally, and add the cauliflower. Cook until the cauliflower is just fork-tender, 5 to 7 minutes. Drain and place the pot back on low heat for 5 minutes to dry the cauliflower out a bit. Be sure to shake the pot every minute or so to ensure that the cauliflower doesn't stick.

Melt half of the butter in a large saucepan and add the bay leaves, garlic and thyme. Lower the heat and cook 3 minutes. Add the flour all at once and stir with a wooden spoon until the mixture is smooth. Continue to cook for another 2 minutes to remove the raw flour taste. Add the vermouth and stir—the sauce will thicken quickly. Next add the milk 1 cup at a time, stirring until smooth. Add 2 cups of the Cheddar, the Gruyère, 2 teaspoons of the salt to taste, and the pepper and stir until the cheese has melted and the sauce is smooth.

To make the topping, melt the remaining ½ stick of butter in a small saucepan or in the microwave. Mix the bread crumbs, remaining Cheddar, and parsley together in a bowl. Add the melted butter and stir well with a fork.

Butter a casserole dish and put the cauliflower into it. Pour the sauce over all. Cover with the crumb topping and place the dish on a baking sheet to catch any drips. Bake in the top half of the oven until the topping has browned, about 20 minutes. Serve immediately.

moody blues

Music is the backbone of every event and is essential in setting the mood for the evening. I wouldn't presume to tell you exactly what to play, since musical taste is so personal. But I will give you some thoughts on what I feel works best.

When hosting a morning breakfast for weekend guests, you can't go wrong with classical. I remember when I was in my early twenties and I'd eat breakfast while listening to new wave music at top volume . . . those days are long gone. Classical music in the morning is like a little ear massage.

A casual brunch gets light folksy music and easygoing vocals. Easy listening may not be at the top of my list throughout the day, but it's an amiable match for a Mimosa. In my mind cocktail parties are set in swanky stone. Since the cocktail party is the only event that actually has its own genre of music, we play cocktail music without fail. Ella Fitzgerald, Billie Holiday, Etta James, Cole Porter, and Frank Sinatra are always the first guests to arrive.

And there is definitely a place for boisterous dance music. The party you throw with a self-serve bar, your closest friends, and finger foods call out for loud beats and elbow room.

Lastly, I think background music can make or break a dinner party. When conversation is intimate, play something fresh and unexpected like world music or jazz. But steer clear of wordy music! There is nothing I find more distracting than listening to a song and singing along in my head.

To go one step further, I invite all of America to join me in my moratorium on playing show tunes at parties. If I can keep just one show queen from playing *Annie Get Your Gun* during a nice meal, this book will have been worth it.

Fennel, carrot, and apple slaw

Most everyone has a traditional slaw recipe. It usually contains cabbage and mayo and that's great—I have one too. But one summer night we had some friends over for a cookout, and I wanted something lighter. This slaw has an incredibly fresh, slightly sweet flavor that's a great complement to grilled meats.

Whisk the lemon juice, honey, sugar, salt, and hot sauce together in a small bowl until the honey dissolves. Add the oil in a steady stream, whisking as you go. Set the dressing aside.

Remove 4 fronds from the fennel, chop them coarsely, and put them in a large bowl. Trim the fennel bulb, quarter it, slice it thinly, and add it to the bowl. Stir the dressing a couple of times to recombine and pour half of it onto the fennel. Toss well.

Core and cut each apple into 1-inch dice. Add the apples and carrots to the fennel and toss.

Stir the dressing again to recombine, then pour it into the slaw and toss well. Refrigerate the slaw for 30 minutes to let the flavors meld before serving.

Yield: 6–8 servings
Preparation time: 20 minutes
Inactive time: 30 minutes

¼ cup fresh lemon juice
2 tablespoons honey
1 tablespoon sugar
1 teaspoon kosher salt
1 teaspoon hot sauce
1 cup vegetable oil
1 fennel bulb, with fronds
3–4 carrots, coarsely shredded
1 red Delicious apple
1 Granny Smith apple

chilling wine

You can chill your wine or champagne in the fridge in 3 or 4 hours, but for speedier results, I recommend using a bucket filled with ice and water. You can even speed up the process by tossing a small handful of salt into the bucket. This is useful to know when you hear the doorbell and realize you've forgotten to chill the wine (but I know that's never happened to any of us). The salt reduces the temperature of the ice to below zero and will get you a chilled bottle in less than 15 minutes. Finally, repeat after me: "I will never leave wine to chill in the freezer." This will cause an imbalance in the alcohol and change the flavor.

rustic onion pie

Yield: 12–18 pieces
Preparation Time: 30 minutes
Cooking Time: 1½ hours

CRUST

4 cups all-purpose flour, plus additional for kneading

2 tablespoons extra-virgin olive oil, plus additional for the pan and brushing the crust

½ teaspoon kosher salt

FILLING

¼ cup extra virgin olive oil

15 anchovy fillets (optional)

4 pounds Spanish onions, peeled and thinly sliced

2 teaspoons kosher salt

2 teaspoons freshly ground black pepper

SPECIAL EQUIPMENT

10-by-15-inch sheet pan

MAKE AHEAD

Pie can be made the day before and refrigerated, covered in foil. Bring back to room temperature before serving.

This is a recipe my grandmother brought with her from Italy back in the 1920s, but I've always thought of it as Augie's onion pie. My mom makes it every year for our family Christmas gathering, and, before he passed, my Uncle Augie would stand at the door, waiting for us to arrive. When we walked in, he'd slap me and pinch my cheeks really hard—that's endearing if you're Italian. Then he'd grab the onion pie from my mother's hands and make off to the kitchen with it. When dinner was served, the onion pie would appear on the buffet with at least half missing. My mother wised up to his tricks pretty quickly and started bringing an extra pie every year, which she'd keep in the car until dinnertime.

Put the flour in a large mixing bowl. Make a well in the center and add the oil and salt and stir to combine. Measure out 1¼ cups warm water and slowly add it to the bowl, stopping just when a dough begins to form (you may only need about a cup of water for this). Turn the dough out onto a well-floured surface and knead until smooth. Divide it into two balls, flatten them into disks, and refrigerate them, well wrapped, until ready to use.

Preheat the oven to 325 degrees F.

Warm the olive oil in a large pot over medium heat for 1 minute. Add the anchovies, if you're using them, and cook, stirring, until they dissolve. Add the onions, salt, and pepper, stir, and cover. Cook, stirring occasionally, until the onions are translucent, 20 to 30 minutes. Set aside to cool.

Remove the dough from the refrigerator and let it come to room temperature. Flour a surface well and roll out one of the disks to about ⅛ inch thick. Grease the sheet pan with olive oil and line it with the dough. Spread the filling out over the dough, roll out the second disk to the same thickness, and place it over the onions. Crimp the edges, brush the whole surface of the pie with olive oil, and cut vent slits into the top.

Bake the pie in the top half of the oven until the dough is golden brown, about 1 hour. Serve the onion pie at room temperature.

Pictured on page 126

tomatillo cheddar cornbread

Cornbread is a natural accompaniment to chili, so try this with the Grilled Chicken and White Bean Chili (see page 111). I think you'll like the zing that's added by the tomatillos and onions.

Preheat the oven to 425 degrees F. Spray the cake pan with nonstick cooking spray.

Pour 1 tablespoon of the butter into a small skillet and place over medium heat. Add the tomatillos, sliced onion, 1 teaspoon of the salt, and a generous amount of black pepper and cook until soft, about 5 minutes.

In a large mixing bowl, combine the cornmeal, flour, baking powder, baking soda, remaining 1½ teaspoons salt, the cayenne, and the sugar. In a separate bowl, whisk together the buttermilk, eggs, and remaining melted butter. Pour the buttermilk mixture into the flour mixture, stirring until well combined.

Fold in the Cheddar and the tomatillo mixture and pour the batter into the prepared pan. Bake the cornbread in the top half of the oven for 30 minutes, until the center is firm to the touch and top is golden. Remove from oven, let cool, and slice.

butter

You would never put a half-eaten sandwich in front of your guests, so why is it okay to put out that hacked-up stick of butter with toast crumbs in it? Making an attractive butter plate is next to no work, and since next to no work is next to godliness, let's jump right in.

First freeze your stick of butter; this makes it easier to cut and handle. Cut slices at a ¼-inch thickness. Take those butter squares and cut them again, this time diagonally. Angle your butter triangles on top of each other on a butter plate. Cut a larger stack for a communal butter plate or, for individual plates, place two triangles and a fresh roll at each guest's spot. Steal the old restaurateur's trick of garnishing with a bit of chopped fresh parsley or snipped chives.

This is another extremely simple tip that awards huge visual impact.

Yield: 8–10 servings
Preparation time: 15 minutes
Cooking time: 35 minutes

---

4 tablespoons (½ stick) unsalted butter, melted

½ cup diced tomatillos (½-inch dice)

1 small yellow onion, thinly sliced

2½ teaspoons kosher salt

Freshly ground black pepper

1½ cups yellow cornmeal

½ cup all-purpose flour

2 teaspoons baking powder

1 teaspoon baking soda

½ teaspoon cayenne

3 tablespoons sugar

1½ cups buttermilk

2 eggs

12 ounces sharp Cheddar, grated (about 1½ cups)

SPECIAL EQUIPMENT

9-inch square cake pan

Nonstick cooking spray

moroccan olive flatbread

Yield: 8–10 servings
Preparation time: 20 minutes
Cooking time: 20 minutes

1 cup plus 1½ tablespoons all-purpose flour, plus additional for kneading

2 teaspoons sugar

Kosher salt

¼ teaspoon freshly ground black pepper

10 oil-cured olives, pitted and chopped

1 tablespoon extra-virgin olive oil, plus additional for the baking sheet and for brushing the flatbread

½ teaspoon garlic powder

¼ teaspoon curry powder

¼ teaspoon paprika

¼ teaspoon ground cumin

MAKE AHEAD

Flatbread can be made the day before—store in a paper bag in a dry place.

My grandmother used to keep little bowls of oil-cured olives in her kitchen, and everyone would snack on them, kind of like the Italian version of peanuts—although, actually, they were most likely Moroccan. The olives made their way into southern Italy via Sicily, which was a crossroads between Italy and Africa. I think their sharp saltiness and purple-black color make this bread a winner.

Put the flour, sugar, 1 teaspoon salt, the pepper, and the olives in a large mixing bowl and stir to combine. Add the olive oil and stir vigorously with a fork. Add ½ cup water and continue to stir until a ball forms.

Sprinkle a work surface liberally with flour, turn the dough out onto the surface, and knead until it is velvety smooth, about 2 minutes. Wrap the dough in plastic and refrigerate for at least 1 hour.

Preheat the oven to 400 degrees F. Coat a baking sheet with olive oil. In a small bowl combine all the spices and ½ teaspoon salt.

Remove the dough from the refrigerator and flatten it into a disk on a floured surface. Using a rolling pin, roll the dough out as thinly as possible into an oval. Loosely roll the dough onto the pin and transfer it to the baking sheet.

Brush the dough with olive oil and sprinkle it with the spice mixture. Bake the bread until it is crisp and deep golden brown, about 20 minutes. Remove it from the oven, let cool, and break it into irregular pieces or serve whole so your guests can break it apart.

Herb and onion Flatbread

When I first moved to Chicago, I worked for a small caterer in the posh northern suburbs. She would make beautiful flatbreads to send to every party and often would send one or two extra as a hostess gift. When The Hearty Boys became so busy that I could no longer work with her, I took the idea of the flatbread with me. I created my own recipe and was surprised at how easy it is to make these beautiful breads. Try it . . . and feel free to steal the hostess gift idea!

Put both flours, the sugar, and 1 teaspoon of salt in a large mixing bowl and stir to combine. Add the olive oil and stir vigorously with a fork. Pour in ½ cup water and continue to stir until a ball forms. Sprinkle a work surface liberally with flour, turn the dough out onto it, and knead until the dough is velvety smooth, about 3 minutes. Wrap in plastic and refrigerate for at least 1 hour.

Preheat the oven to 400 degrees F. Coat a baking sheet with olive oil.

Remove the dough from the refrigerator and flatten it into a disk on a liberally floured surface. Using a rolling pin, roll the dough out as thinly as possible into an oval. Roll the dough loosely onto the pin and transfer it to the baking sheet.

Brush the dough with extra-virgin olive oil and sprinkle with the onion, rosemary, thyme, sage, garlic powder, 1 teaspoon of salt, and the pepper. Bake the flatbread until it is crisp and deep golden brown, about 20 minutes. Remove it from the oven, let cool, and break it into irregular pieces or serve whole so your guests can break it apart.

Yield: 8–10 servings
Preparation time: 20 minutes
Cooking time: 20 minutes

1 cup all-purpose flour, plus additional for kneading

1½ tablespoons whole-wheat flour

2 teaspoons sugar

Kosher salt

1 tablespoon olive oil, plus additional for the baking sheet and for brushing the flatbread

½ red onion, thinly sliced

Leaves from 2 rosemary sprigs

Leaves from 3 thyme sprigs

8 whole sage leaves

1 teaspoon garlic powder

½ teaspoon freshly ground black pepper

MAKE AHEAD

Flatbread can be made the day before—store in a paper bag in a dry place.

desserts

Ionce waited tables in a very "in" New York restaurant in the theater district. I loved it. We didn't get a lot of tourists, but we did get all the stage actors and crew. I loved knowing everyone involved in the shows, the backstage gossip, and the free tickets I'd get when they were "papering the house." It was our own little off-Broadway theater in there, complete with a campy host who yelled at me once for seating an important celebrity before he was able to greet the person. "I'm no longer an actor. This is now my stage," he said, wagging his long finger at me. "I'm the star here. . . . *Don't* step on my dress."

I used to like to come into the restaurant between auditions and help in the kitchen. Our dessert menu was locally renowned, and I'm proud to say my lemon brown sugar bread pudding was one of our top sellers. In fact, since the shows would end fairly late in the evening, many performers would come in just for coffee and sweets. Actually, that's a half truth, the coffee was rarely served without a shot of something from the bar. They were actors after all.

Anyway, we had a lot of fun with the celebrities who came in after the shows. I particularly remember one well-known comic asking me where his bread pudding order was.

"Shoot," I said. "I'm sorry." I shrugged and smiled at him. I knew he really didn't mind . . . after all, we're all in the same business, right? We're all kindred souls trodding the boards, struggling to get our name in lights on the great white way. What's a little missed dessert between amigos? "I must have forgotten it." I let out a little rueful laugh I knew my brother-in-arms would understand. "I guess that's why I'm an actor."

"That's great," my comrade replied, leveling me with a look. "So why don't you try acting like a waiter?"

raspberry fool

Yield: 6–8 servings
Preparation Time: 20 minutes

10-ounce package frozen raspberries in syrup, thawed

2 cups heavy whipping cream, chilled

6 tablespoons confectioners' sugar

1 pint fresh raspberries

1 pint fresh blackberries

1 mango, peeled and sliced

6–8 fresh mint sprigs, for garnish

SPECIAL EQUIPMENT

6–8 martini glasses (see note)

Chilled bowl

Before we all start making jokes about this dessert, let me just say that the name derives from the French word *foule* which means "pressed" or "crushed." It refers to the mixture of fruit puree and cream, and a lighter, easier, more sublime dessert can't be found.

Puree the frozen raspberries using a blender or food processor.

Pour the heavy cream into a chilled bowl and, using an electric mixer, beat it until it begins to thicken. Stop the mixer, add the sugar, and continue to beat on high until firm peaks form when the mixer is lifted from the cream.

Gently fold ⅓ cup of the raspberry puree into the whipped cream. Do not mix too well, as you want swirls of the raspberry in the cream.

Pour a small amount of the remaining raspberry puree into the bottom of the serving glasses. Mound about 3 large tablespoons of fool onto the puree. Chill the desserts up to 8 hours if you are not serving them immediately.

Just before serving, top the fool with the fresh berries and mango and garnish with mint sprigs.

COOK'S NOTE: Any stemmed glass with a wide mouth makes a dramatic presentation.

cardamom shortcake with maple berries

Shortcake pairs perfectly with berries, and most any spice or flavoring can be mixed into the batter. For this recipe, I chose cardamom, with its warm, eucalyptus-like notes. Experiment with adding your own spices.

Preheat the oven to 375 degrees F.

Combine the flour, ½ cup of the sugar, baking powder, cardamom, and salt in a mixing bowl. Add 1¾ cups of the heavy cream and mix until a dough forms. Put the dough onto a floured surface and pat it into a disk 6 inches in diameter. Cut into six wedges and place on an ungreased baking sheet. Brush each wedge with the remaining 3 tablespoons of cream and sprinkle with the remaining 2 tablespoons of sugar

Bake the shortcakes in the top half of the oven for 25 minutes, until they are golden and firm to the touch. Remove the shortcakes to a baking rack to cool.

While the shortcakes are baking, put the berries and maple syrup in a bowl. Let the fruit macerate until you're ready to assemble the desserts.

Slice each shortcake in half and place the bottom halves on a platter or on individual dessert plates. Divide the berries among them. Cover with the short-cake tops and garnish with whipped cream.

Yield: 6 servings
Preparation time: 15 minutes
Cooking time: 25 minutes

---

2 cups all-purpose flour, plus additional for the work surface

½ cup + 2 tablespoons sugar

2 teaspoons baking powder

1 teaspoon ground cardamom

½ teaspoon kosher salt

1¾ cups + 3 tablespoons heavy cream

2 pounds strawberries, hulled and quartered

1 cup maple syrup

Whipped cream, for garnish

Bananas Foster with chocolate crème fraîche pot

Yield: 8 servings
Preparation time: 10 minutes
Cooking time: 10 minutes

3 cups crème fraîche

15 ounces semisweet chocolate, chopped

Bananas Foster, recipe follows

Cocoa powder, for garnish

SPECIAL EQUIPMENT

8 individual 6-ounce soufflé cups

MAKE AHEAD

Chocolate Crème Fraîche Pots can be made the day before and chilled overnight.

I've always loved the pairing of rich chocolate and bananas. When we opened HB, I created this slightly tart, very chocolaty dessert topped with warm, velvety spiced bananas. I like the illusion of its being a fancy dish that takes a lot of time to prepare, when in reality it takes minutes. The ganache itself needs at least an hour in the refrigerator, so as it's chilling, you'll have time for the more important things—like a cocktail.

Warm the crème fraîche in a medium-size saucepan over medium heat. Stir until it begins to bubble, then add the chopped chocolate. Stir well until the chocolate melts and the mixture becomes smooth. Pour into the soufflé cups and chill, covered, for at least 1 hour. Just before serving, prepare Bananas Foster.

Bananas Foster

½ cup (1 stick) unsalted butter

1 cup light brown sugar

2 teaspoons cinnamon

8 ripe bananas, peeled and sliced on the bias into 1-inch pieces

1 cup banana liqueur

1 cup rum or brandy

Melt the butter in a large skillet over high heat. Add the sugar and cinnamon and stir until the sugar dissolves, about 3 minutes. Add the bananas and stir gently to coat.

Remove the pan from the heat and add the liqueur and rum carefully. Return the skillet to the heat and allow the liquid to come to a simmer. Using a long match, flame the liquor. Allow the flames to die out on their own. Spoon the bananas over the chocolate ganache and dust with cocoa powder. Serve immediately. Yield: 8 servings

white chocolate risotto with orange ganache

Yield: 8–10 servings
Preparation time: 10 minutes
Cooking time: 20–30 minutes

6 cups whole milk, plus
additional if needed

½ cup sugar

1 teaspoon ground nutmeg

Peel of 1 orange (see note)

½ cup dried tart red cherries

½ cup brandy

2 tablespoons unsalted butter

2 cups Arborio rice

8 ounces good-quality white
chocolate, chopped

Orange Ganache,
recipe follows

1 can mandarin orange
segments, drained, for garnish

White chocolate shavings,
for garnish

It's funny that when we think of rice pudding we always think of long grain white rice—right? Arborio is higher in starch than white rice so it's naturally creamier, which makes it a no-brainer for rice pudding. I tried this recipe out on a group of friends one night and, hands down, they all loved the rich, creamy texture, the subtle white chocolate flavor, and the chewiness of the tart cherries. It's another recipe that you can make your own by the addition of different dried fruits or even flavoring agents such as rose water or almond extract.

Pour the milk into a large saucepan and add the sugar, nutmeg, and orange peel. Set the pan over high heat and bring the milk to a simmer before reducing the heat to low.

Put the cherries into a small saucepan with the brandy and ¼ cup water and simmer until the cherries plump up, about 10 minutes.

Meanwhile, melt the butter in a second heavy-bottomed saucepan over medium heat. Add the rice and stir well to coat. Add 1 cup of the hot milk to the rice and stir constantly until most of the liquid has been absorbed. Continue to add the milk by the cupful, stirring constantly, until the rice is still firm, but not crunchy to the bite. This will take 15 to 20 minutes. (If the rice is still crunchy after that, heat more milk and add it by the half cupful.) Stir in the white chocolate and the cherries and continue to cook until the chocolate has completely melted. Remove the pan from the heat and set aside. When cool, chill it in the refrigerator for at least 2 hours or overnight (see note).

For a dramatic presentation, divide the risotto into martini glasses using an ice cream scoop. Drizzle with the ganache and garnish with mandarin orange segments and white chocolate shavings.

COOK'S NOTE: When removing the peel from the orange, use a sharp paring knife and cut in a circular motion, being careful to leave most of the pith behind.

orange ganache

8 ounces semisweet chocolate chips

1 cup heavy cream

2 tablespoons triple sec or other orange liqueur

This is the cheater's way of making ganache. Place the chocolate and cream in a glass or plastic bowl. Microwave the mixture on high for 1 minute, then remove and stir. If necessary, return the ganache to the microwave for 30 seconds. As you stir, the chocolate should incorporate into the cream, creating a smooth texture. Add the triple sec and stir well until combined. Serve immediately. Yield: 1½ cups

caffeine rush

I hate to leave the action at the dinner table because I live in fear of missing out on something. I'm told it's because I'm a Gemini, but I think it's because my friends critique my clothes and hair as soon as I leave the room. So, I quickly clear the dishes and get back in there ASAP.

A simple trick that has boosted my speed is to include the coffee service in my prep work. While I set the table or finish chopping vegetables, I grind coffee beans and put them into the filter, fill the coffee maker with water, prefill the creamer, top off the sugar bowl, and pre-plate a few packets of sweetener. This way, all I have to do is pile the used dishes in the sink, hit "brew," and rush back to the table while my reputation is still intact.

MAKE AHEAD

Risotto can be made the day before and refrigerated in an airtight container.

Lemon Brown Sugar Bread Pudding with Blueberry Cream

Yield: 6–8 servings
Preparation time: 25 minutes
Cooking time: 30 minutes

What's not to love about bread pudding? It's warm, soft, sweet, and creamy—a truly comforting dessert perfect for a chilly night. This is my favorite—Steve will make it occasionally for just the two of us. The tart lemon flavor topped with the blueberry cream is a knockout.

Preheat the oven to 350 degrees F.

Put bread cubes into a large bowl. In a second large bowl, combine the eggs, cream, brown sugar, lemon zest, and vanilla and pour the mixture over the bread. Mix well and let sit for at least 15 minutes so the bread can absorb the custard mix.

Butter a casserole dish and pour the bread pudding into it. Bake it in the top half of the oven until the center is slightly firm to the touch, about 30 minutes. Serve warm, topped with chilled Blueberry Cream and garnished with a few fresh blueberries and a sprinkle of confectioners' sugar.

1 loaf challah bread, cut into 1-inch dice

6 eggs, beaten

2 cups heavy cream

1 loosely packed cup light brown sugar

Zest of 2 lemons

1 teaspoon vanilla extract

Blueberry Cream, recipe follows

½ cup fresh blueberries, for garnish

Confectioners' sugar, for garnish

Blueberry Cream

1½ cups sour cream

½ cup frozen blueberries, thawed

¼ cup light brown sugar

1 teaspoon vanilla extract

Put all the ingredients into a blender or food processor and process until smooth. Refrigerate until ready to use. Yield: 2½ cups

MAKE AHEAD

Bread pudding can be made the day before and reheated.

Blueberry cream can be made the day before.

amaretto profiteroles

Yield: 40 profiteroles
Preparation Time: 1 hour
Cooking time: 50 minutes

¾ **cup (1½ stick) unsalted butter, softened**

¼ **teaspoon kosher salt**

1 cup all-purpose flour

5 eggs

Slivered almonds

Amaretto cream, recipe follows

SPECIAL EQUIPMENT

Cooking spray for the pan

The holiday season, as we all know, is more than a little hectic. Throw in a busy catering business and "insane" would be the better description. Keeping that in mind, I had just finished a sheetpan's worth of these profiteroles for some friends' gift baskets. My brother, Bob, was hanging out in the kitchen with me while I baked them, and as I was standing there, full sheet pan in hand, our six-month-old kitten leaped from the floor to the counter to the center of the pan.

Profiteroles went flying. I immediately had a meltdown, and Steve, running into the kitchen, tried to be helpful by saying that there were three that could be salvaged. "What's the point?" I ranted. "I've got to do the whole #$@% thing over again!"

Still trying to be helpful, he said, "Well, three is better than none." At that, I truly went off the deep end. I yelled about the crazy cat, how much work I had to do that night, how nobody understood me, yada, yada . . . you get the picture, right? After about 5 minutes of this, Bob leaned over and flattened the remaining three profiteroles with his fist—*boom, boom, boom*! I'll tell you what— it broke the tension, and I don't think we've ever laughed so hard.

Preheat the oven to 375 degrees F. Spray a baking sheet with nonstick cooking spray. In a small bowl, beat 1 of the whole eggs with 1 teaspoon water and set aside.

To prepare the puffs, combine 1 cup water with ½ cup of the butter and salt in a large saucepan and bring to a boil over high heat. Reduce the heat to medium and add the flour all at once. Stir the mixture with a wooden spoon until it begins to pull away from the sides of the pan and forms a ball. Transfer the mixture to the bowl of a standing mixer and, with the mixer on high, beat in the 4 remaining whole eggs, one at a time, making sure to beat well after each addition. The batter should be stiff enough to just hold soft peaks.

Immediately spoon the batter into a pastry bag fitted with a ½-inch pastry tip and pipe puffs about 1½ inches in diameter by 1 inch high onto the baking sheet. Brush the top of each puff with the egg wash and sprinkle with slivered almonds. Bake the puffs in the top half of the oven for 20 to 30 minutes, or until they are golden. Remove them from the oven, pierce the side of each puff with a sharp knife. Turn the oven off and return the puffs to the oven for an additional 20 minutes to dry. Remove from the oven after the 20 minutes and transfer to a rack to cool.

To assemble the profiteroles, fill the pastry bag with the amaretto cream. Using a serrated knife, cut each puff in half horizontally. Pipe the cream ¾ inch high onto the base of each puff. Cap with the tops and refrigerate until ready to serve.

amaretto cream

2 cups whole milk

6 large egg yolks

½ cup sugar

⅓ cup cornstarch

3 tablespoons amaretto

Bring the milk to a boil in a small pot over high heat, then reduce the heat to low and let simmer.

Put the egg yolks, sugar, and cornstarch into a pot and whisk well. Slowly add a quarter of the hot milk into the egg mixture, whisking the whole time. Add the remaining milk in a steadier stream, continuing to whisk. Place the pot over medium heat and let the mix come to a boil, whisking constantly. Continue to whisk and cook for 1 minute longer. Remove the mixture from the heat and pour it through a fine strainer into a bowl.

Place the pastry cream bowl into a larger bowl filled with ice and continue to stir for 1 minute. Add the butter a tablespoon at a time, whisking well after each addition to make sure the cream is smooth. Add the amaretto and whisk well to combine. Place a piece of plastic wrap directly onto the surface of the pastry cream and allow it to chill completely before using. Yield: 2¾ cups

MAKE AHEAD

Profiteroles are best served the day they are assembled.

Pastry cream can be made the day before.

rustic apple tart

Yield: 8 servings
Preparation time: 40 minutes
Cooking time: 1 hour

6 Granny Smith (or other firm, tart) apples, peeled and cored

½ cup sugar, plus additional for sprinkling the crust

2 tablespoons dry sherry

1 tablespoon fresh lemon juice

1½ teaspoons ground cinnamon

¼ teaspoon ground allspice

¼ teaspoon ground ginger

⅛ teaspoon ground nutmeg

Flour, for rolling the dough

1 recipe Pâte Sucrée, recipe follows

2 tablespoons unsalted butter, cut into bits

2 tablespoons heavy cream, for brushing the crust

I love the look of this tart—the apples are mounded in the center of the pastry dough and then it's gently folded up around them, leaving the center open so that the uncovered apples get golden brown. The bonus is that if you're not great at crimping pie dough, like me, the tart will still be beautiful.

Preheat the oven to 350 degrees F.

Cut each apple into twelve segments and put them in a large mixing bowl. Add the sugar, sherry, and lemon juice and toss to coat well. Add the cinnamon, allspice, ginger, and nutmeg and mix well. Set aside to let the flavors blend for 15 minutes.

On a well-floured surface, roll the dough out into a 15-inch circle. Transfer this to a baking sheet and mound the apples in the center, leaving the juices behind. Make sure to leave a generous 2-inch border all the way around. Dot the apples with the butter and fold the dough border up around the apples. (It won't meet in the center.) Brush the dough with cream and sprinkle with sugar.

Bake the tart in the bottom third of the oven for 30 minutes, then transfer it to the top third for an additional 30 minutes. Let cool for 15 minutes before serving.

pâte sucrée

1¼ cups all-purpose flour, plus additional for the work surface

1 tablespoon sugar

⅛ teaspoon kosher salt

7 tablespoons unsalted butter, chilled and cut into bits

½ cup water with ice

Pour the flour, sugar, and salt into the bowl of a food processor and pulse to combine. Add the butter and pulse until the mixture resembles coarse crumbs. With the processor running, add the ice cold water 1 tablespoon at a time, until a dough just begins to form. (You should need about 3 tablespoons water.)

Turn the dough out onto a lightly floured surface and pat it into a disk. Wrap it in plastic and refrigerate for at least 20 minutes. Yield: 15-inch crust

rosewater cupcakes with Grenadine frosting and sugared rose petals

Yield: 24 small cupcakes
Preparation Time: 45 minutes
Cooking Time: 20 minutes

1¾ cups all-purpose flour

2 teaspoons baking powder

¼ teaspoon kosher salt

3 large eggs

1½ cups sugar

¾ cup whole milk

2 tablespoons rosewater
(available in specialty food
stores or online)

6 tablespoons unsalted
butter, melted

1 teaspoon vanilla extract

Grenadine Frosting,
recipe follows

Sugared Rose Petals, for
garnish, recipe follows

SPECIAL EQUIPMENT

24-compartment mini muffin tin

Pastry bag with #32 star tip

Rosewater, which is truly made from distilling rose petals in water, has long been a predominant flavoring in Arabic cuisine. A thirteenth-century Arabian cookbook called for the use of rosewater in over 60 percent of its recipes—and yet, it's still a relatively unknown flavoring agent in western cooking. It adds a flowery, delicate note to these cupcakes and makes them a perfect summer dessert.

Preheat the oven to 350 degrees F. Coat the muffin tin with cooking spray and set aside.

Mix the flour, baking powder, and salt together in a small bowl and set aside.

In a large bowl, beat the eggs with the sugar until the mixture turns a pale yellow. Add the dry ingredients and beat until smooth.

Bring the milk and rosewater to a boil in a small pan (or heat the mixture in a microwave set on high for 2 minutes). Add the hot milk to the batter in a slow stream, beating until well combined. Stir in the butter and vanilla. Beat until well combined.

Pour the batter into the muffin tin, filling each compartment three quarters of the way. Bake the cupcakes until the tops are golden and the surface springs back when touched, 15 to 20 minutes. Remove from the oven and let cool for 10 minutes in the tins. Turn out onto a rack and let cool completely.

To assemble the cupcakes, put the frosting into the pastry bag. Pipe frosting onto the top of each cake in a spiral pattern, starting from the outside and working in, to form a peak in the center. Place a rose petal standing up in the center of each cupcake.

Pictured on page 151

grenadine frosting

1 pound cream cheese, at room temperature

½ cup (1 stick) unsalted butter, at room temperature

1 cup confectioners' sugar

½ teaspoon vanilla extract

1 tablespoon grenadine

Put the cream cheese and butter in the bowl of a mixer and, using the paddle attachment on high, beat until well incorporated. Add the sugar and beat 1 minute longer. Add the vanilla and grenadine and beat until the frosting is a uniform pink. Refrigerate, covered, until ready to use. Let the frosting come to room temperature before using. Yield: 1 pint

sugared rose petals

24 pesticide-free rose petals (pink, red, yellow, or a combination)

2 egg whites, lightly beaten

1 cup sugar

Using a pastry brush, brush the petals with the egg whites and roll them in the sugar, making sure to coat both sides. Lay them on a wire rack and allow them to dry for at least 2 hours. Yield: 24 rose petals

chocolate cream cheese cupcakes

These are one of Steve's favorites. They're evocative of the Hostess cream-filled chocolate cupcakes we had as kids, but everything about them is better. The cake is moist; the filling is creamy, sweet, and studded with chips; and the frosting is rich and slightly tangy.

Preheat the oven to 350 degrees F. Place paper liners in the muffin tin.

Combine the flour, 2 cups of the sugar, cocoa, salt and baking soda in a large mixing bowl. Pour 2 cups water, the oil, vinegar, and vanilla into a second bowl. Slowly pour the wet ingredients into the dry, using a whisk to mix them as you pour. Continue to whisk until the batter is smooth, 1 to 2 minutes. Pour it into the prepared muffin cups, filling them three quarters of the way.

Put the cream cheese and remaining ⅓ cup sugar into the bowl of a mixer and whip until smooth. Add the egg and whip until the mixture is light. Fold in the chocolate chips. Drop 1 tablespoon of the cream cheese mixture into the center of each cupcake. Bake the cupcakes in the top half of the oven until the cake springs when touched, about 20 minutes. Let cool in the tin before frosting.

For a homey look, use a butter knife to spread the cream cheese frosting. For a fancier look, use a piping bag with a star tip. Begin at the edge of the cupcake and pipe the frosting in a spiral motion toward the center of the cupcake. Lift the pastry bag up at the center to form a peak.

cream cheese frosting

1 pound cream cheese, softened

½ cup (1 stick) unsalted butter, softened

2 cups confectioners' sugar

1 teaspoon vanilla extract

Put the cream cheese and butter into the bowl of a mixer and beat until well combined, 1 to 2 minutes. Add the sugar 1 cup at a time, beating after each addition. Add the vanilla extract and beat 1 minute longer. Yield: 2½ cups

---

Yield: 24 cupcakes
Preparation time: 25 minutes
Cooking time: 20 minutes

3 cups all-purpose flour

2⅓ cups sugar

½ cup cocoa powder

2 teaspoons baking soda

1 teaspoon kosher salt

⅔ cup vegetable oil

2 tablespoon cider vinegar

2 teaspoons vanilla extract

8 ounces cream cheese, softened

1 egg

8 ounces semisweet chocolate chips

Cream Cheese Frosting, recipe follows

SPECIAL EQUIPMENT

12-compartment muffin tin

Paper muffin liners

MAKE AHEAD

Unfrosted cupcakes can be made the day before and stored in an airtight container.

Frosting can be made up to 3 days in advance and stored, covered, in the refrigerator. Let soften to room temperature before using.

steve's espresso shortbreads

Yield: 9–12 pieces of shortbread
Preparation Time: 20 minutes
Cooking Time: 20 minutes

¾ cup (1½ sticks) unsalted butter, at room temperature

½ cup sugar

½ teaspoon vanilla extract

1½ cups all-purpose flour

1½ tablespoons espresso powder

¼ cup espresso beans, roughly ground

SPECIAL EQUIPMENT

9-inch square baking pan

Cooking spray

Steve made these shortbreads for me as a birthday surprise one year. It was one of the nicest presents I've ever gotten because, when you cook for a living, people tend to be afraid to cook for you. These are buttery, as all good shortbreads should be, and they pack a huge coffee flavor. They've become a favorite in our house. We make them whenever friends are coming by—but unfortunately we've usually eaten them all before our friends get here!

Preheat the oven to 350 degrees F. Coat the baking pan with cooking spray and set aside.

Cream the butter and sugar together until light and fluffy. Add the vanilla and mix for 30 seconds. Add the flour and espresso powder and mix until the dough is smooth, about 1 minute.

Press the dough evenly into the prepared pan. Scatter the espresso beans over the top and press lightly. Bake the shortbread in the top half of the oven until it is set, 18 to 20 minutes. Remove from the oven, score so that it will cut neatly and let cool for 15 minutes.

Run a butter knife around the edge of the pan and invert it over a cutting board. Give one sharp rap, and the shortbread will release from the pan. Let cool an additional 10 minutes and slice along the scored lines.

coffee bar

If you're offering coffee at a buffet or sideboard, take this tip to give your event a coffeehouse feel. Along with the coffee urn, we put out shakers of powdered sugar and cocoa, bowls of chocolate shavings, and flavored coffee syrups. Chilled bowls of fresh whipped cream are always a hands-down hit. Simply refrigerate a metal or glass bowl so that when you fill it with freshly whipped cream it stays cooler longer on the buffet . . . more innovative than a milk pitcher!

I'm a black-coffee guy myself, but hey, the chicks go wild for this stuff.

biscotti regina (sesame seed cookies)

One of my earliest food memories: I'm sitting at the blue boomerang–patterned Formica table in my grandmother's kitchen. She's taking trays of sesame seed cookies that she's always called Biscotti Regina (from the old country) out of the oven and letting them cool on the counter before handing me one. I dunk it in the coffee milk that she's set in front of me. Some of the seeds fall off and float in the drink. The life of a four-year-old is good.

Preheat the oven to 350 degrees F.

Combine the flour, baking powder, and salt in a bowl and set aside.

Put the butter and sugar into the bowl of a mixer and cream until fluffy. Add the eggs, one at a time, with the mixer running, and beat until smooth. Add the vanilla and beat. Add the flour mixture and beat until well incorporated.

To form the cookies, divide the dough in half and roll it into two logs 1 inch in diameter. Cut the logs into 1½ inch lengths. Pour the cream into a shallow dish and sprinkle the sesame seeds on a plate.

Dip each piece of dough into the cream and then roll it in the sesame seeds. Bake the cookies on an ungreased baking sheet until golden brown, 15 to 20 minutes. Let cool on baking sheet before serving.

Yield: 30 biscotti
Preparation time: 30 minutes
Cooking time: 20 minutes

4 cups all-purpose flour

1 tablespoon baking powder

½ teaspoon kosher salt

1 cup (2 sticks) unsalted butter, at room temperature

1 cup sugar

3 eggs

1 teaspoon vanilla extract

1 cup heavy cream

2 cups sesame seeds

watch your butt!

We aren't smokers, but occasionally we'll be at an event where there are heavy smokers. Nothing spoils my appetite like seeing ashtrays filled with cigarette butts. The rule of thumb is that you should never see more than two butts in a tray. Use this old waiter's trick for cleaning an ashtray: Place a clean ashtray upside down over the dirty one before you pick it up. This way you can scoop the offending tray off the table without leaving a mini tornado of ash. The simple restaurant/bar-quality glass ashtrays are perfect for this.

MAKE AHEAD

Can be made up to 2 weeks in advance and stored in an airtight container.

libations

When we entertain, we always have cocktail "courses." I like starting the party off with a classic cocktail, pouring wine with dinner, and ending the night with an after-dinner drink that pairs with dessert or stands on its own if need be. Our guests appreciate a planned drink menu, and they've come to expect me to make unusual offerings.

We had clients over for a light supper one night. It was one of those beautiful summer days that makes you somehow feel fit and want to eat healthy. So, instead of offering dessert we went European with an after-dinner cheese course. We had moved outdoors to the patio, and I thought icy cold yet spicy hot martinis were in order. I pulled the pimientos out of oversized olives and replaced them with a hearty slice of pickled jalapeño. Then, after adding a touch of vermouth to the shaker along with the vodka, I dirtied it up with a splash of jalapeño juice from the jar.

Our guests sipped their cocktails on the deck while I finished slicing up fresh baguettes and cheeses. By the time I came out with the platter the group had gone a bit quiet and our friend, Isaiah, was pondering his martini glass. "Hmmm," he said looking up at me, "I wasn't expecting the vanilla in this. . . . It's interesting." Horrified, I realized I had grabbed a bottle of vanilla vodka out of the liquor cabinet! I snatched glasses from everyone's lips and rinsed out the cocktail shaker.

What I love about this story, though, is that had Isaiah not made mention of the taste, my polite guests would have finished drinking their vanilla jalapeño martinis (the recipe for which will not be found in this chapter). God bless our friends. They all blindly trust that we know what we're doing!

Goccia di Limone

Yield: 1 cocktail

1 ounce vodka

1 ounce limoncello

1 ounce pomegranate juice

¼ ounce fresh lime juice

1 lemon wedge, for garnish

We based this drink on the Lemon Drop; a newcomer in comparison to some of the other cocktails we're featuring, but a classic nonetheless. It introduced in the 1970s in a San Francisco singles bar and can be enjoyed as a martini or a shooter. We gave ours an Italian kick by using limoncello and pomegranate. Of course, since the pomegranate is hailed for its antioxidants you may want to enjoy this cocktail as a health tonic. Cincin!

Combine the liquid ingredients in a cocktail shaker filled with ice. Shake well. Strain into a martini glass, garnish with the lemon wedge, and serve.

The Vesper

Yield: 1 cocktail

2 ounces Bombay Sapphire gin (see note)

1¼ ounces vodka

½ ounce Lillet blanc

"I never have more than one drink before dinner. But I do like that one to be large and very strong and very cold and very well made. I hate small portions of anything, particularly when they taste bad. This drink's my own invention."

—JAMES BOND

The name and recipe for this cocktail come from *Casino Royale*, the first Bond novel, by Ian Fleming. As you know, of course, the Vesper should be "shaken not stirred." The shaking serves two purposes; a colder martini and better vermouth incorporation, both of which result in a smoother cocktail. We've chosen it because it uses Lillet, a French aperitif that everyone should experience firsthand. Lillet is in the vermouth family and is bottled in both white and red versions. Purchase white Lillet for this recipe. I recommend that you also try a glass over ice with a slice of fresh orange!

Combine the liquid ingredients in a cocktail shaker with ice. Shake well and strain into a martini glass. Twist the lemon peel over the drink, rub it around the rim, drop it in the drink, and serve.

COOK'S NOTE: I prefer the subtleties of Sapphire and find that its herb blend mellows the juniper flavor that can sometimes be too strong in gin.

TALK WITH YOUR MOUTH FULL

pomegranate sour

Back in the 1920s and '30s, many cocktails were made with egg whites for the froth they added. The silky, luxe feel on the tongue isn't bad either! Our sour is a riff on the traditional whiskey sour. Of course, if raw eggs are a problem, you can use pasteurized egg whites, which are usually found in a carton near the dairy section at the grocery store.

Place all the ingredients except the lime slice in a cocktail shaker with ice and shake vigorously until foamy. Serve in a Collins glass over ice with the lime for garnish.

Yield: 1 cocktail

2 ounces pomegranate liqueur
½ ounce grenadine
1 ounce fresh lime juice
1 egg white
Slice of lime, for garnish

french 75

No classic drink menu would be complete without a champagne cocktail. This one is named after an artillery field gun from World War I that was so technologically advanced it was used through WWII. Because of the gin, this little cocktail, like the big gun, packs quite a wallop.

Shake the gin, lemon juice, and sugar in a cocktail shaker with ice. Top with about 2 ounces of the Prosecco and stir gently. Pour into a champagne glass and garnish with a long lemon twist—the longer the better.

Yield: 1 cocktail

1 ounce gin
1 ounce fresh lemon juice
2 teaspoons sugar
Prosecco or sparkling wine
Strip of lemon zest, for garnish

real cuba libre

Having worked as a bartender at numerous catered events, I thought I knew what this was: rum and Coke with a squeeze of lime and—*boom!*—Cuba Libre, right? Wrong! The added burst of the lime zest is critical. This is what the drink should taste like—smooth and refreshing.

Zest the lime half into a tall Collins glass and squeeze the juice into the glass as well. Drop the lime hull in and add the rum. Stir, add ice, fill with cola, and serve.

Yield: 1 cocktail

½ lime
1½ ounces light rum
Cola

Gingered Lemonade,
recipe follows

Chilled pale ale or
light lager

lemon shandy

Lemon shandies, a combination of lemonade and ale (I know, sounds odd but it's tasty!), are extremely popular in England. In fact, we spent one Christmas with Steve's Aunt Sheila in the Cotswolds, and after she'd put the turkey in the oven, we went to the local pub to meet with her friends and neighbors. We drank shandies and sang Christmas carols, drank shandies and played darts, drank shandies and told stories. I don't remember much about the turkey, but I do remember those shandies. We've spiced up our version with fresh ginger—you'll love it!

Fill a pint glass two thirds of the way with ale and top with the lemonade. Serve ungarnished, as the English do.

gingered lemonade

1 lemon

1 cup sugar

Six ½-inch coins fresh ginger

1 cup fresh lemon juice

Using a sharp knife, cut the zest off the lemon, leaving as much of the white pith behind as possible, as this will cause the lemonade to taste bitter.

Put 1 cup water, the sugar, lemon peel, and ginger into a saucepan and bring to a boil over high heat. Stir to dissolve the sugar and remove the pan from the heat. Allow to cool, remove the peel and ginger, and add the lemon juice along with 2 cups water. Chill the lemonade before using. Yield: 1 quart, enough for about 10 shandies

aviation cocktail

This drink was popular in the 1930s when aviation was all the rage—back when people were all excited about Charles Lindbergh being the first pilot to cross the Atlantic and Howard Hughes's prototype cargo plane, the *Spruce Goose*. The cocktail faded from view when maraschino liqueur lost its popularity and gin was replaced by vodka as the liquor of choice. Buy yourself a bottle of maraschino, though, and familiarize yourself with its peppery nuttiness. You'll be surprised to find that it's only slightly sweet with hints of cherries. We've bumped up the amount in our cocktail to give it a more a contemporary taste.

Combine the ingredients in a cocktail shaker filled with ice. Shake well. Strain into a martini glass, garnish with a cherry, and serve.

Yield: 1 cocktail

2 ounces gin
1 ounce maraschino liqueur
½ ounce fresh lemon juice
Maraschino cherry, for garnish

waste not, want not

I love to introduce my guests to "lost" and vintage cocktails—as a conversation spark as well as a bonus "frugality factor." When I find half a bottle of maraschino liqueur, or rarely used liquors like crème de cassis or Pimms taking up space in my cabinet, I do some quick recipe research to find a signature drink that features that ingredient. A small gathering is an ideal time to dress up your bar with forgotten favorites like La Floridita daiquiris, Pimm's Cups, and Vesper martinis. Many vintage drinks have intriguing back stories and you'll find that guests are always interested in a little booze trivia. At least, they seem interested to me, but that may be because I'm picking up the tab.

rosemary peach cosmopolitan

Yield: 1 cocktail

As much as I love a good Cosmo, they're starting to feel a little been-there, done-that. We thought we'd up the ante a bit by adding fresh herbs. The combination of the rosemary and peach feels great on the tongue and leaves a nice, long finish on the palate.

Fill a cocktail shaker with ice. Add all the liquid ingredients and shake well. Strain into a martini glass and serve garnished with the rosemary sprig.

2 ounces Absolut Apeach or similar peach vodka

¾ ounce Rosemary Syrup, recipe follows

½ ounce white cranberry juice

½ ounce fresh lemon juice

Rosemary sprig, for garnish

rosemary syrup

2 cups water

½ cup sugar

4 sprigs fresh Rosemary

Put the water and sugar into a saucepan and place over high heat. Bruise the rosemary by laying it on a cutting board and pounding it with the handle of a knife. This will release the essential oils. Put the sprigs into the saucepan. Bring to a boil and stir to dissolve the sugar. Lower the heat to medium and simmer until reduced to 1½ cups, about 8–10 minutes. Remove from the heat and let cool. Strain and store in the refrigerator until ready to use.

comparing apples to appletinis

Let's do some math—I'll do it for you!—and compare the cost of beer and wine to spirits. An affordable bottle of decent wine will cost in the neighborhood of $12. We get five glasses from a bottle, which comes to $2.40 per drink. A six-pack of imported beer runs about ten dollars, or $1.66 per drink. A bottle of name-brand vodka, however, will cost about $20.

Now, if a standard 750-milliliter bottle yields 16 drinks at a cost of $1.25 per drink, what can we conclude? Full bars can actually be more cost-effective than you realized. Or as my grade-school math teacher would have said, "Beer and wine > full bar."

2 ounces tequila

1 ounce triple sec

4 ounces Hibiscus Tea, recipe follows

Lime wedge, for garnish

Granulated sugar

Hibiscus Margarita

We were at a summer party at the house of our friends, Quincy and Nando, when Quincy brought out these beautiful, deep-red drinks that were slightly tart but sweet and totally addictive. Later in the evening, I cornered him in the kitchen and got the recipe out of him. Hibiscus flowers (or "Jamaica," as they're known in Mexico) are often used for iced tea, and that's the base for this cocktail. My recipe makes a gallon of the tea. You might not use it all for margaritas, but you'll want to drink it alone over ice.

Fill a cocktail shaker halfway with ice. Add the tequila, triple sec, and tea and shake hard. Rub the rim of a margarita glass with the lime and dip the rim into the sugar. Fill the glass with ice and pour the margarita into the glass. Garnish with the lime wedge and serve.

Hibiscus Tea

2 cups dried hibiscus flowers (see note)

3 cups sugar

½ cup fresh lime juice

Bring 1 gallon water to a rolling boil in a stockpot over high heat. Add the hibiscus, remove from the heat, and let the mixture steep for 15 minutes. Pour the tea through a strainer, pressing down on the solids. Discard the solids, add the sugar and lime juice, stir well, and let cool. Pour into a pitcher and refrigerate until cold before using. Yield: 1 gallon

COOK'S NOTE: Hibiscus flowers can be found in Latin supermarkets or natural food stores.

pimm's cup

Yield: 1 cocktail

2 cucumber slices

1 lemon slice

2 apple slices

2 ounces Pimm's No. 1

6 ounces good-quality lemon soda, such as San Pellegrino Limonata

Pimm's No. 1 is an English gin-based spirit which contains quinine and a secret herb mixture. I first tasted this cocktail in our friend Mike's backyard (must have missed it at the pub in the Cotswolds—too busy sucking down lemon shandies, see page 174.) The cucumber, although something we're not used to dropping into our cocktails here in the US, is traditional and adds an amazingly fresh twist.

Fill a tall Collins glass or double rocks glass with ice and add the cucumber, lemon, and apple slices. Pour the Pimm's over the fruit first and then add the soda; stir and serve.

keeping it cool

Ice buckets look great on a bar, but they are often too small and impractical for larger get-togethers. In their place, we've used large, deep, silver mixing bowls (in excellent condition), clear Lucite buckets, and even Igloo coolers wrapped in cloth. It's easy to find ice bucket substitutes in everything from copper tubs to deep vintage ceramic bowls to colorful children's beach pails, if you use your imagination. Just be sure that whatever you use is waterproof and sturdy enough to withstand chipping and icy temperatures.

You'll need something to scoop the ice, of course. There are plenty of inexpensive ice tongs available, but tongs annoy me because I can only pick up one or two cubes at a time. I prefer an ice scoop. The little metal ones are readily available in housewares stores and are a fundamental addition to a bar kit. And, remember: *never* use a glass to scoop ice. A small chip of clear glass mixed in with the ice is a major health hazard. If you ever break or chip a glass in your ice, you must pour it all away; no exceptions.

pegu club

Yield: 1 cocktail

2¼ ounces gin

1 ounce Cointreau, or other orange-flavored liqueur

¾ ounce fresh lime juice

3 healthy dashes Angostura bitters

Lime slice, for garnish

This cocktail is named after a British officers' club that existed in Burma in the late 1800s. It was popular worldwide (the cocktail, not the club). When Burma gained its independence, the club closed and the drink fell into obscurity. We introduced it to one of the couples who won *The Food Network Caters Your Wedding*, and they wisely made it the signature drink for their reception. This tasty cocktail is almost like a gin margarita—and it deserves to be resurrected.

Pour all the liquid ingredients into a cocktail shaker filled with ice and shake well. Strain into a martini glass, garnish with the lime slice, and serve.

cold beers

The best way to chill beer and wine is to use those plastic tubs you find at housewares stores. *Before* adding ice, place the beer bottles on their sides, stacking like brands together. Organizing brands that way eliminates the "beer fishing" of college days. A few of your white wine bottles (preopened, with the corks loosely set back in) should also be placed upright at one end of the tub. Only then should you pour the ice directly over the bottles. Cold air travels down and will soon be followed by shifting cubes and ice-cold melting water. This is how we ice down beers at catered events, and it cools them in 30 to 45 minutes.

This tub can be placed behind the bar if you have a bartender, or on a self-serve bar itself if you are using a large (and sturdy) table. Either way, wrap the tub in a tablecloth to give it a more decorative look.

Another important note: Always use a plastic tarp or trash bag under the cloth to protect your bar table or floor from condensation.

2 ounces white rum

1 ounce fresh lime juice

1 teaspoon sugar

¼ ounce maraschino liqueur

Lime wedge, for garnish

La Floridita

This cocktail was created during Prohibition at the bar in Havana of the same name. It was Ernest Hemingway's hangout, and he drank them frozen (see note). The cocktail fell out of favor when Castro took over Cuba, and we're more than happy to help reintroduce it. As you make this delightful cocktail, you might think it's kind of like a daiquiri—and you'll be right. But it's a daiquiri as it should be.

Pour all the ingredients except the lime wedge into a cocktail shaker filled with ice and shake well. Strain over crushed ice into a double rocks glass, garnish with the lime wedge, and serve.

BARTENDER'S NOTE: To serve the cocktail frozen, put 1 cup ice into a blender along with the other ingredients. Blend on high until smooth.

1¾ ounces vodka

½ ounce fresh lime juice

3 ounces ginger beer
(see note)

Moscow Mule

Pictured opposite

This cocktail gave vodka a big boost in the 1950s. As legend would have it, it was invented at a bar on Sunset Boulevard by a representative of Smirnoff vodka, then a struggling company, and a gentleman whose ginger beer company was faltering. They served it in cool copper mugs, which have since become collector's items, and found that they had an immediate hit on their hands.

Fill a double rocks glass (or copper mug, if you've got it) with ice. Add the vodka, lime juice, and ginger beer. Stir well and serve.

COOK'S NOTE: Ginger beer is the stronger, spicier cousin to ginger ale. Substituting will leave you with a weaker taste.

Yield: 8–10 servings

6 English Breakfast tea bags

½ cup honey

6–8 fresh mint sprigs, plus additional for garnish

3 cups lemonade

6 ounces Absolut Citron (or other lemon vodka)

1½ ounces peach schnapps

Honey Lemon Tea Punch

We feel that punch has gotten a bad rap due to the fact that it too often seems to be a runny blend of rainbow sherbet and lemon lime soda (OK, so maybe we're partly to blame for spreading that negative press). Tea based punches, however, are marvelous additions to a buffet dinner. This recipe has all the comfort based memories of curling up with a warm honey and lemon toddy. But by taking those yummy flavors, adding a little more citrus, a hint of peach, and serving them chilled, we've got a great punch—sweet, tart, and perfect with grilled foods.

Pour 6 cups water into a large saucepan and bring to a boil over high heat. Remove from the heat, add the tea bags, honey, and mint sprigs and let steep for 30 minutes. Discard the tea bags and mint, straining the tea through cheesecloth, if necessary. Chill before continuing.

When the tea is chilled, pour it into a punch bowl. Add the remaining ingredients and 2 cups ice cubes. Serve over ice, garnishing each glass with a mint leaf.

Yield: 8 servings

4 herbal apple tea bags

1 teaspoon whole cloves

¼ cup sugar

1 cup cranberry juice

½ cup apple juice

1 cup Captain Morgan's Spiced Rum (or other spiced rum)

¼ cup applejack whiskey

1 apple, sliced into rings, for garnish

Apple Picker's Punch

When I was a kid, we'd often take trips to upstate New York, which is apple country. I can remember going apple picking and then, as we paid for the fruit in the barn/gift shop, my parents would buy a couple of gallons of fresh-pressed cider. Back at home, my dad would mix up a spicy apple drink, spiked for my mom and himself, virgin for us. I've taken those tastes and created a punch that pairs beautifully with the Cider Braised Pork Roast (see page 99).

Bring 4 cups water to a boil in a large saucepan and add the tea bags and cloves. Remove from the heat and let steep for 5 minutes. Add the sugar, stir to dissolve, and let cool to room temperature. Strain and chill before using.

Pour the tea, cranberry juice, apple nectar, rum, and applejack into a punch bowl, garnish with the apple rings, and serve.

wicked tea

We call this one wicked because it's a greenish color—just like the Wicked Witch of the West! You'll be surprised at how easily this goes down. It's refreshing because the tea is unsweetened, and it's a great drink to have with the Pan Fried Soft Shell Crabs (see page 114).

Bring 3 cups water to a boil in a large saucepan and add the tea bags. Remove from the heat and let steep until cool, about 20 minutes. Chill before continuing.

Pour the green tea into a punch bowl along with the rum, Midori, grape juice, and ginger ale. Garnish the punch bowl with honeydew balls and serve

Yield: 6–8 servings

3 green tea bags
¾ cup Bacardi Apple rum
¼ cup Midori
¾ cup white grape juice
1½ cup ginger ale
Honeydew balls, for garnish

a punch list

- Use fresh juices whenever you can; pulpy fruits like oranges and limes add texture to the punch.
- Tart flavors stimulate the appetite more than sweet so use unsweetened juice when possible.
- Tea punches actually complement the flavors of the food and are better matches with dinner menus. The balance is smooth and layered without the heavy sweetness that deadens the taste buds.
- Be sure to offer a nonalcoholic version as well for those who don't imbibe. Substitute apple cider for apple rum, peach nectar for peach schnapps, cran-raspberry juice for crème de cassis, etc.
- Add your bubbles (club soda, ginger ale, prosecco) right before your guests arrive.
- Premix and refrigerate extra batches to top off your punch bowl during the party. This saves time and ice because a chilled beverage stays cool longer. In fact, freezing small batches of the punch to use in place of ice is a great way to keep summer drinks cold without diluting them!

rum refresher

This punch is the grown-up version of Southern sweet tea, and it's aptly named because it's really refreshing. Try it at a picnic with fried chicken.

Combine 2 cups water, the sugar, and the mint in a saucepan and bring the mixture to a boil over high heat. Stir to dissolve the sugar and remove the pan from the heat. Let the syrup cool, strain to remove the mint, and refrigerate it until ready to use.

Mix all the ingredients in a punch bowl and chill until ready to serve. Garnish with fresh mint leaves.

Yield: 8 servings

1 cup sugar

6–8 sprigs fresh mint, plus additional for garnish

1½ cup Meyers dark rum

4 cups black tea

2 cups orange juice

El diablo punch

Pictured opposite

The El Diablo is a fruity tequila cocktail which we love. We figured that if one glass is yummy, a bowl full must be heavenly so we used it as the basis for a punch. We've lightened it with the addition of white grape juice for a sweet, tangy punch that really packs a punch!

Pour all the liquid ingredients into a punch bowl and stir to combine. Float the lime hulls in the punch as garnish.

Yield: 6–8 servings

1½ cups silver tequila

1 cup crème de cassis

2 cups white grape juice

2 cups ginger ale

Juice of 4 limes, hulls reserved for garnish

the iceman leaveth

You'd be shocked at how much ice we go through at big receptions. Most clients think of only how much ice is needed to fill the mixed drink glasses, forgetting that we need to put ice in each guest's water glass, continuously fill cocktail shakers and still have enough to chill wine, beer, and champagne.

Caterers order three pounds of ice per guest for large events. Again, it depends on what you'll be serving at your bar and how you're planning to chill the bottles (if you have enough refrigeration space), but even home parties require about a pound and a half per guest. You should remember that running out of ice (and you know you always do) means you have to abandon your guests and do the dreaded ice run.

1 cup whole shelled almonds

1 teaspoon almond extract

4 black tea bags

¼ cup sugar

1 cup silver tequila, chilled

½ cup triple sec, chilled

1 cup orange juice, chilled

1 cup guava nectar, chilled

SPECIAL EQUIPMENT

Fluted Bundt pan

ponche Almendrado (Almond punch)

When we were in Mexico, we had some delicious drinks as we sat by the edge of the ocean. The unusual thing in a couple of them was the almond flavor. I was never able to find out whether it was a liqueur or just extract. I tried to re-create one of them when we got home, and here's what I came up with—it's a little tropical with an Aztec feel, and the ice ring is just a lot of fun.

To make the ice ring, scatter the almonds on the bottom of the Bundt pan and fill it halfway with water. Stir in ½ teaspoon of the almond extract and freeze the ring until solid, about 8 hours.

Bring 4 cups water to a boil, add the tea bags, and steep for 5 to 7 minutes. Remove the tea bags. Stir in the sugar while the tea is still hot. Let it cool and chill until ready to serve.

Just before serving, combine all the liquid ingredients in a punch bowl and float the almond ring on the top.

popping a cork

The "aim and push" method of popping a champagne cork is best reserved for Super Bowl victories and hot tub parties. At best, you might leave a mark on your ceiling; at worst you could take out somebody's eye. But even more importantly, when you forcefully pop a cork, you lose the heart of the champagne: its bubbles. The French have a saying for that: "The ear's gain is the palate's loss." But, of course, when they say it, it's in French.

The simple solution is to place a dish cloth over the cork and champagne neck as you open the bottle. Do this as soon as you remove the wire cage from the cork (better yet, loosely drape the cloth over the bottle before you remove the wire). While gripping the cork tightly through the cloth, twist the bottle, not the cork, and lastly, don't grip the neck of the bottle for very long. This warms the glass, and the temperature difference between cold champagne and a warm bottle neck leads to fizzing. And fizzing, as we all know, leads to wasted champagne. And wasted champagne leads to . . . well, it just leads to sadness, doesn't it?

red bubbles

Here's the perfect punch to serve at a brunch. It's light, effervescent, and slightly sweet, but the dominant note is the wonderful bitterness of Campari.

Pour all the liquid ingredients into a clear pitcher, stir gently, and serve immediately in champagne glasses garnished with lemon twists.

Yield: 8–10 servings

4 cups champagne, chilled
½ cup Campari
1 cup seltzer, chilled
1 cup red grape juice, chilled
8 strips lemon zest, for garnish

piña colada punch

I should have known I was destined to be a caterer when I showed up at beer parties in high school with a blender in hand and the makings for piña coladas in my backpack. That's an embarrassingly true story for a couple of reasons—which I have now shared with all who read this cookbook.

I no longer travel with a blender under my arm, but I do still have a fondness for piña coladas. This version is slightly less sweet than most and goes really well with spicy foods.

Whisk the coconut cream with 1 cup water until smooth and pour it into a punch bowl, along with the rums and pineapple juice. Top with pineapple soda and seltzer just before guests arrive and stir for frothy texture. Float the pineapple icebergs large side down (cherry side up) in the punch bowl.

Yield: 10–12 servings

1 cup cream of coconut
1 cup coconut rum
½ cup dark rum
2 cups pineapple juice
4 cups pineapple soda
1 cup seltzer
Pineapple Icebergs,
recipe follows

pineapple icebergs

18 maraschino cherries
12 ounces pineapple juice

SPECIAL EQUIPMENT: **12-compartment muffin tin**

Fill six compartments of the muffin tin three quarters of the way with pineapple juice and add 3 cherries per tin. Freeze overnight. Just before you're ready to serve the punch, run warm water over back of the tin to release the bergs. Yield: 6 bergs

thai iced coffee punch

Yield: 10–12 servings

2 cups cold black coffee

6 cups hot strong black coffee

6 teaspoons espresso powder

1½ cups sweetened condensed milk

¾ cup vanilla ice cream

1 cup vanilla vodka

¾ cup dark rum

¼ teaspoon ground cardamom

This recipe is strongly reminiscent of the real thing but with a lighter consistency. That means I can drink more of it! I'll be up all night bouncing off the walls but at least I'll feel less full. Think of this punch first for holiday get-togethers and dessert parties. You'll be very happy.

Pour the cold coffee into an ice cube tray and freeze overnight.

Mix the hot coffee with the espresso powder and sweetened condensed milk. Add the ice cream and mix until melted. Add the vodka, rum, and cardamom and stir. Refrigerate for at least 1 hour. Add the coffee ice cubes right before serving.

ruby apple

Pictured opposite

Yield: 10–12 servings

3 cups fresh ruby red grapefruit juice

¾ cup calvados

¾ cup curaçao

¾ cup apple juice

750 ml bottle of Prosecco

¾ cup seltzer

Grapefruit supremes from one ruby red grapefruit (see page 26), for garnish

I love the color and sweet-tart taste of ruby red grapefruits. Combined with sparkly Prosecco and sweet apple juice, they make for a punch that is an all-around winner at brunches, lunches, and summer cookouts.

Pour the grapefruit juice, calvados, curaçao, and apple nectar into a pitcher and chill for at least 1 hour. When ready to serve, transfer the mixture to a punch bowl and add the Prosecco and seltzer. Garnish the punch bowl with the grapefruit supremes and serve immediately.

wait at the bar

Keep in mind that people naturally like to gather around a bar, so put it where guests can comfortably congregate. One of the most common mistakes I see at parties is having both the bar and the buffet in the kitchen. Guests get trapped in the one room while other useful spaces around the house remain mostly empty. Although this can be comical, I still like to create a flow at a party by giving guests a reason to move about. A bar in the dining room, snacks in the living room, live music on the sun porch, buffet in the kitchen . . . you get the idea.

blush sangria

Yield: 6–8 servings

750-milliliter bottle White Zinfandel, or other fruity white wine

¼ cup strawberry liqueur

½ cup peach nectar

1½ cup lemon lime soda

1 peach, pitted and cut into 8 slices

1 cup fresh strawberries, sliced

Steve originally put this pink sangria together for our friend Tonya's surprise baby shower. Twenty of our friends came over, decorated the backyard, and put out a massive selection of potluck foods. Steve even baked a baby shaped lemon cake with coconut hair and a pacifier. Our big mistake was in not letting her husband in on the plans because at 8 months pregnant, Tonya made a last minute decision to turn off her phone and put her feet up. Adults: 20; Babies: 0. Oh well, we all enjoyed this sunny sweet sangria and still managed to save her the "head half" of the baby cake!

Pour the wine and rum into a large pitcher and add the lemon and lime slices and cherries. Refrigerate for 6 hours. Add the soda, strawberries, and ice to the pitcher and stir. Serve immediately.

black sangria

Yield: 8-10 servings

750-milliliter bottle fruity red wine

¼ cup triple sec

½ cup crème de cassis

1 cup cranberry juice

Scant ½ cup fresh squeezed lemon juice

1 pint fresh raspberries

1 pint fresh blackberries

A basic sangria is a carnival of color; blending wines, sweet juices and a myriad of fruits including tart citrus. I wanted to offer a sangria recipe that would be completely different, so I honed in on what I love most about this Spanish punch. This lush sangria is an inky blend of rich flavors and the best of the dark berries of high summer. I like to think this is what crimson tastes like.

Pour the wine, triple sec, crème de cassis, cranberry juice, and lemon juice into a large pitcher. Add the fruit and refrigerate for 6 hours. Stir and serve over ice.

apricot punch with basil floats

This is our homage to the vintage ice cream punch recipes. The Campari counteracts the sweet nectar while the basil sorbet (which is also great for a palate cleanser or even dessert) adds an unexpected herbal zing. When assembling the punch, make sure the small scoops of sorbet are frozen solid before adding them to the cold liquid—they'll last longer. Oh, and did I mention how excited your guests will be with the combination of fruit and herbs?

Pour all the liquids into a punch bowl and garnish with the basil floats. Serve immediately.

basil floats pictured at right

½ cup **sugar**

½ cup **Sauvignon Blanc**

10–15 fresh basil leaves, chopped coarsely

SPECIAL EQUIPMENT: **Melon baller**

Combine ½ cup water, the sugar, and the wine in a saucepan and bring to a boil over high heat. Lower the heat and simmer for 5 minutes to dissolve the sugar. Remove from the heat and let cool.

Pour the cooled mixture into a food processor, add the basil, and blend well. Transfer to a shallow pan and freeze until mostly firm but still a little slushy. Scrape the sorbet into the food processor and pulse to break up any chunks. Refreeze until the sorbet is almost solid again, about 2 hours. Use the melon baller to make the basil float scoops and freeze them until solid before using them in the punch. Yield: 25-30 basil floats

Yield: 8–10 servings

2 cups **apricot nectar**

1½ cups **ginger ale**

3 cups **Prosecco**

½ cup **Campari**

¼ cup **fresh lemon juice**

Basil Floats, recipe follows

Angel's Tit

Pictured on page 171

Yield: 1 cocktail

Maraschino cherry

1½ ounces maraschino liqueur

¾ ounce heavy cream or half-and-half

Let me just say right up front that I can't take credit for this drink's name. It was given its dubious moniker during Prohibition, when it was one of the most popular liqueur drinks. Name aside though, it's both delicious and strikingly beautiful.

Drop the maraschino cherry into a sherry glass. Pour the liqueur into the glass and gently pour the cream into the glass over a spoon so that it floats on the top.

Irish Pirate

Yield: 1 milk shake

½ cup whole milk

½ pint green mint chocolate chip ice cream

½ teaspoon pure mint extract

1½ tablespoons dark rum

Mint sprig, for garnish

Every year Steve waits for Saint Patrick's Day to come around so he can get Shamrock Shakes from McDonald's. They're one of his favorite things— no comment! Anyway, I thought I'd try to recreate one for him but wound up going off on a tangent and created this really yummy milk shake with a kick instead. Steve says he'll take the Pirate over the Shamrock any day—personally I think that's because there's booze in it.

Put the milk, ice cream, mint extract, and rum into a blender. Blend on high until smooth, about 15 seconds. Pour into a chilled glass and garnish with a sprig of mint.

Sunny Irishman

Yield: 1 cocktail

Freshly brewed coffee

½ ounce Cointreau or other orange liqueur, or to taste

½ ounce Irish whiskey, or to taste

Whipped cream

Green crème de menthe, for garnish

This is a riff on traditional Irish coffee—we call it sunny because the orange makes us smile.

Fill a mug most of the way with hot coffee. Stir in the orange liqueur and Irish whiskey. Add a dollop of whipped cream and drizzle with crème de menthe.

chocolate espresso with candied orange peel

My family always has to have espresso after a big meal. We call it "black coffee" as opposed to, say, French roast, which is "brown coffee." Initially Steve didn't know this so when my mother asked if he wanted black coffee he naturally said yes, expecting to get his normal big mug of coffee without cream and sugar. He was quietly disappointed by the teeny espresso cup set in front of him. Last Christmas we came up with this espresso drink. It's chocolaty, a bit sweet, and gets a hint of citrus from the whipped cream. The candied orange zest is fun to nibble as you sip the espresso.

Whisk the cream until soft peaks form. Add the triple sec and continue to whisk until firm peaks form. Refrigerate until ready to use.

Pour the Godiva into an espresso cup and fill the rest of the way with espresso. Top with a dollop of the whipped cream and serve with the candied orange zest on the side.

candied orange zest

Ten 1½-inch-long strips of jaggedly cut orange zest, white pith left behind

1 cup sugar plus more for rolling zest in

Place the orange zest into a saucepan and cover with water. Bring to a boil, reduce the heat, and let simmer for 5 minutes to soften the zest. Drain, add 1 cup of water and 1 cup sugar to the pan along with the zest, and return to the heat. Stir to dissolve the sugar and let simmer until the zest begins to turn translucent, about 8–10 minutes. Drain and roll each piece of zest in extra sugar. Set aside to dry for at least 1 hour. Can be kept for 3 days in an airtight container. Yield: 10 pieces

Yield: 1 cocktail

¾ ounce Godiva chocolate liqueur

Espresso

1 cup heavy cream

2 tablespoons triple sec

Candied Orange Zest, recipe follows

pomegranate thyme cordial

I created this cordial for a series of cooking classes I did a few years back. Along with each class's theme, I created an original drink. I love toying with the marriage of fresh herbs and cocktails and this one got rave reviews. Prepare it for a holiday meal—it's a perfect ending to a Thanksgiving dinner.

Combine the pomegranate juice, sugar, and thyme in a medium-sized saucepan over high heat. When the mixture begins to boil, stir it and reduce the heat to medium. Let the liquid simmer until it's been reduced by half, about 15 minutes. Remove it from the heat and let it cool.

When the syrup has cooled to room temperature, strain it through cheesecloth into a large bowl. Stir in the wine and vodka and transfer the cordial to a glass carafe or decanter. Let it mellow for at least 2 days before serving.

Serve in cordial glasses with a few pomegranate seeds as garnish.

Yield: about 1 quart

2 cups pomegranate juice

¾ cup sugar

6 sprigs fresh thyme

2 cups white Zinfandel

1 cup vodka

Fresh pomegranate seeds, for garnish

how many glasses?!

I'm just going to come out and say it: You need three glasses per guest for your cocktail party. Before you argue, I want you to think of how often you go to a party and wander around saying, "What did I do with my wine glass?" before giving up and getting a fresh one.

If you have a bar stocked with wine, beer, and mixed drinks, you will need a mix of glassware that amounts to three glasses per guest. I recommend using just two types: an 8-ounce all-purpose wineglass and a 13-ounce double rocks glass (add martini and champagne glasses for more involved bars).

If you have the storage, you might want to invest in a case of inexpensive stemware for the occasional large event like New Year's Eve. They run about three bucks each from restaurant supply stores and wholesale club warehouses; just be sure to save the box they came in to store them between parties. A case will last a lifetime, and the occasional broken stem will be no big deal when compared to risking your good stuff. Plus, let's be honest, do you really trust your friends with your good crystal?

1 ounce brandy

¾ ounce crème de cacao

½ ounce hazelnut liqueur such as Frangelico

1 ounce heavy cream

Freshly grated nutmeg, for garnish

1 ounce brandy

1 ounce dry vermouth

½ ounce curaçao

¼ ounce Campari

1 ounce scotch

1 ounce butterscotch schnapps

1 ounce amaretto

Nutty Alexander

A Brandy Alexander is a riff on the Alexander cocktail, a gin based drink that has its roots in Prohibition. It may seem odd to pair gin with cream, but the cream hid the harsh taste of the speakeasy moonshine. The Brandy Alexander, with its warm and silky charm, soon became the more famous brother. But for our taste, it's almost too smooth and milky; it calls out for a touch of nut. Our version adds Frangelico.

Pour all the ingredients into a cocktail shaker filled with ice and shake vigorously. Strain into a martini glass and sprinkle nutmeg on top.

The Diablo

The Diablo cocktail can be called an aperitif and enjoyed before a meal, but I think the bitter Campari (bitters are said to aid digestion) and brandy make this a prime after-dinner drink. You may have noticed that we've also included the El Diablo punch (page 187) in this chapter—similar names but completely different drinks. After dinner, move your guests away from the dining table and into the living room. Get comfy on the couch and enjoy the warmth and sweetness of this classic cocktail.

Pour all the ingredients into a cocktail shaker filled with ice. Shake well and strain into a martini glass.

Butternut Scotch

Every after-dinner drink selection should offer one over-the-top-sweet candy-type drink. This is our pick. Think of it as a butterscotch Manhattan!

Pour all the ingredients into a rocks glass filled with ice. Stir and serve.

financier

This drink was inspired by the little tea cakes you find in sidewalk cafés in Paris. They're traditionally made with almond and are sometimes topped with fruit. The combination of pear and almond sounded irresistible as we were experimenting with this drink, and indeed, that proved to be true!

Pour all the ingredients into a cocktail shaker filled with ice and shake well. Strain into a cordial glass or cognac glass and serve.

Yield: 1 cocktail

1 ounce dry vermouth

½ ounce amaretto

1 ounce pear eau de vie, such as Poire William

digestivo

The slightly bitter, herby taste of the Averna is balanced by the sweet berry flavor of the cassis and the smokiness of the whiskey. Don't skimp on the lemon twist either—it adds an essential citrus pop at the end.

Fill a double rocks glass with ice. Pour all the ingredients over the ice and stir. Twist the lemon rind over the cocktail. This will release the essential oils. Run the lemon twist around the rim and drop it into the glass.

Yield: 1 cocktail

¾ ounce crème de cassis

½ ounce Averna

½ ounce triple sec

1 ounce Canadian whiskey

Lemon twist

artichoke soda

Cynar is a deep-brown, bittersweet aperitif made from distilled artichokes. Why, you may ask, have we put an aperitif into the digestive section of the book? It's because artichoke is one of the oldest medicinal plants, used by the Egyptians and Romans to aid digestion. But mainly we put it here because we like to serve it on summer nights while playing cards after big grill fests. Don't be put off by the thought of artichoke soda though—the combination of the spicy-herbal ginger beer, sweet, velvety limoncello, and bitter Cynar is intoxicating.

Pour all the ingredients into a rocks glass filled with ice, stir, and serve.

Yield: 1 cocktail

½ ounce Cynar

½ ounce limoncello

2 ounces ginger beer

guinness float

1 tablespoon Stout Syrup, recipe follows, or more to taste

1 scoop vanilla ice cream

1 scoop chocolate ice cream

12-ounce bottle Guinness or other stout

This is an unusual combination that you'll want to pull out every so often to wow your stout-loving friends. As our friend Lee said before he tried this float, "I like Guinness, and I like ice cream. What's not to like?"

Drizzle the syrup into a tall glass. Add the ice creams, top with stout, and serve immediately.

stout syrup

1 cup sugar

12-ounce bottle Guinness or other stout

Combine the sugar and stout in a saucepan and bring to a boil over high heat. Reduce the heat to low and simmer until thick, 8–10 minutes. Let cool before using. Yield: about 1¼ cups

pouring drinks

Guests like a prop to hold when they're at a party. They feel more comfortable with something in their hand, and more often than not, their drink is that prop. So make it easier on them by being judicious with your pours and remembering that no friends will thank you the next day for pouring overly strong drinks. Plastic bottle pourers (available at housewares stores and easily cleaned in the dishwasher) really come in handy at self-serve bars.

Use the bartender's trick of "counting" to approximate how many ounces are in your pour. A bottle with a pour spout pours liquor at about ½ an ounce a second. The standard mixed cocktail (gin and tonic, screwdriver, rum and Coke) has 1.5 ounces of liquor which would be a "three count." To clarify: While pouring with a standard pour spout, count off "one Mississippi, two Mississippi, three Mississippi." (We said "Mississippi" growing up in North Jersey; but if you come from "one one thousand, two one thousand" territory, feel free to substitute).

sample menus with timelines

Rule number one is that good cooks get that way by being creative. In fact, we encourage you to tweak our recipes! But this brings us to rule number two. Only make a substitution because you choose to, not because you are suddenly caught without an ingredient. That mistake is simply and easily avoided by reading through the whole recipe before you begin cooking.

Case in point: We have a friend whose identity should be kept secret. We'll refer to her as Jane and not her real name, which is Karen O'Grady. With her understocked fridge, ingredient substitutions are a free-for-all, and although I can't say much for her cooking prowess, I think she may have a career in chemistry.

I remember one time she tried her hand at poultry. You know that chicken recipe that uses mushroom soup? It's pretty standard fare, fairly difficult to screw up. She grabbed the soup from the pantry, went to the fridge, and got the chicken breasts and a few carrots . . . then she realized she didn't have the necessary sour cream her recipe called for. So she substituted a carton of vanilla-flavored soy milk and fed her unsuspecting husband wet vanilla chicken. Though he had to leave the table, to his credit, he hasn't left the marriage.

We spent Thanksgiving together, and she asked if she could bring a homemade cheesecake. Sucker that I am, I agreed. Of course, halfway through assembling the cheesecake, she realized she didn't have cream cheese. So my pal scoured her cabinets and found something she figured would make a good substitution in her dessert of doom: a box of instant vanilla pudding. I can only assume that she noticed both products are white and made the leap from there. Anyway, after baking the cake and somehow forcing it to gel, she actually fed it to us at Thanksgiving dinner. Needless to say, it hasn't become a holiday tradition.

So, for all the Karens, er . . . Janes out there, here is a chapter on execution. But you should still feel free to play with these menu suggestions and make them your own. Simply remember rule number three. And that is that Vanilla Soy Milk Chicken pairs up with . . . well, pretty much nothing.

Sunday
* Make pot pie filling
* Make blue cheese dip

Monday
* Day of rest!

Tuesday
* Make cupcakes
* Make green goddess dressing
* Make red pepper coulis for salad
* Make lemonade for shandies

Wednesday
* Prepare biscuit topping and bake pot pie
* Roast root veggies
* Assemble salad
* Frost cupcakes

Wednesday
* Make Caesar dressing

Thursday
* Make biscotti
* Make shortbreads

Friday
* Make onion pie
* Prep veggies for confetti
* Make balsamic mushroom sauce for chicken

Saturday
* Sear chicken and bake
* Make rotini
* Roast potatoes
* Sauté vegetable confetti
* Make croutons for salad and assemble

comfort food with friends

Sometimes all I want is a homey meal that instantly takes me back to childhood. When our closest friends or family are coming over, this is the kind of menu I prepare—warm, comforting food that puts everyone at ease.

HORS D'OEUVRES
Blue Cheese and Caramelized Onion Dip (PAGE 62)

DINNER
Chicken Pot Pie (PAGE 106)
Oven-roasted Root Vegetables (PAGE 141)
Iceberg Wedge with Green Goddess Dressing (PAGE 87)

DESSERT
Chocolate Cream Cheese Cupcakes (PAGE 167)

DRINKS
Lemon Shandy (PAGE 174)
White wine: Pinot Gris

An Italian-inspired Buffet Dinner

To me, buffet dinners mean lots of people—and when I'm feeding lots of people, whether at a catered event or at home, I like to give choices. Keep in mind that they'll take a little bit of everything, so cut the portion sizes down a bit. For example, I'd offer 4-ounce portions of chicken rather than 6-ounce ones.

BUFFET DINNER
Balsamic Mushroom Chicken Breasts (PAGE 109)
Baked Rotini with Tomato Cream (PAGE 122)
Oven-roasted Yukon Gold Potatoes (PAGE 128)
Pan-sautéed Vegetable Confetti (PAGE 140)
Hearts of Romaine Caesar Salad (PAGE 86)
Rustic Onion Pie (PAGE 146)

DESSERT
Biscotti Regina (PAGE 169)
Steve's Espresso Shortbreads (PAGE 168)

DRINKS
Digestivo (PAGE 199)
Beer: Peroni Italian Lager

A seated Dinner party

Whenever we throw a dinner party at our house, I keep the focus on the dinner, not the hors d'oeuvres. I usually set out only one small plate (two at the most) before the meal. It gets everyone's juices flowing, so when it's time to sit down, they're ready to shower me with praise for the wonderful food I prepared.

HORS D'OEUVRES
Wine-soaked Figs and Goat Cheese (PAGE 46)

FIRST COURSE
Leek and Cremini Ravioli with Red and Yellow Tomato Concassé (PAGE 72)

MAIN COURSE
Pepper-encrusted Rack of Lamb with Madagascar Green Peppercorn Sauce (PAGE 96)
Herbed Porridge (PAGE 132)
Anise Roasted Green Beans (PAGE 139)

DESSERT
Bananas Foster with Chocolate Crème Fraîche Pot (PAGE 154)

DRINKS
Angel's Tit (PAGE 194)
Red wine: Pinot Noir

sports sunday

There are Sundays when you just want to hang around the house and watch football. If you have some friends over, it just makes the day better. Add some hearty, low-maintenance food to the mix and it becomes the perfect, relaxing day.

MUNCHIES
Spinach, Artichoke, and Bacon Dip (PAGE 55)
Spiced Cocktail Nuts (PAGE 69)

GRUB
Grilled Chicken, White Bean, and Basil Chili (PAGE 111)
Tomatillo Cheddar Cornbread (PAGE 147)

SWEETS
Rustic Apple Tart (PAGE 162)

DRINKS
El Diablo Punch (PAGE 187)
Beer: Samuel Smith's Pale Ale

TIME LINE for Saturday's Party

Thursday:
Make ravioli and freeze

Friday:
Make peppercorn sauce for lamb
Make tomato concassé for ravioli
Make chocolate pot

Saturday:
Make figs and goat cheese
Cook ravioli
Sauté chard for ravioli
Roast lamb
Make porridge
Roast green beans
Make bananas foster

TIME LINE for Sports Sunday

Friday
* Make spiced nuts

Saturday
* Make spinach dip
* Make chili
* Make apple tart

Sunday
* Bake cornbread
* Reheat chili
* Warm apple tart

Sunday
* Make spinach parmesan balls and freeze
* Make pear balsamic drizzle

Monday
* Make cocktail nuts

Tuesday
* Make hummus
* Make pita crisps

Wednesday
* Make tonnato

Thursday
* Boil shrimp

Friday: 30 min. before party
* Bake spinach parmesan balls
* Slice pears and assemble ricotta salata platter

TIME LINE for Sunday Party

Thursday
* Make pita crisps
* Make orange butter for canapés

Friday
* Make sauce for kebabs

Saturday
* Make tabbouleh
* Make vuelve la vida
* Make gazpacho
* Make brioche toasts for smoked salmon canapés

Sunday
* Make caprese mix
* Make and grill kebabs
* Make slaw

pre-event cocktails

Steve and I work so much that we've learned, out of necessity, how to entertain last minute. We'll often have friends over right after work and before heading out to the theater or the movies. At that point, of course, everyone is hungry. I usually set out a few casual hors d'oeuvres to hold everyone over until we get to dinner later in the evening. This menu is brilliant because everything can be prepped beforehand so, when you run into the house late from work (as I always do), there's almost nothing left to prepare, and you look like a fabulous host to your friends!

Rosemary-Scented Hummus with Savory Pita Crisps (PAGES 63 AND 66)
Ricotta Salata with Freshly Sliced Pears and Pear Balsamic Vinegar (PAGE 47)
Fray's Spinach Parmesan Balls (PAGE 39)
Shrimp Tonnato (PAGE 30)
Spiced Cocktail Nuts (PAGE 69)

DRINKS
Pegu Club Cocktails (PAGE 181)
Vodka Martinis

afternoon garden party

Whether you have a large backyard or a small deck, when the weather turns warm, it's great to entertain outdoors. Serve dishes that are best either chilled or at room temperature—it's more refreshing and less work for you during the party.

PASSED HORS D'OEUVRES
Watermelon Gazpacho Shooters (PAGE 41)
Caprese Cups (PAGE 31)
Smoked Salmon Canapés with Orange Butter and Capers (PAGE 34)

BUFFET LUNCH
Middle Eastern Beef Kebabs (PAGE 102)
Vuelve la Vida, served in demitasse cups (PAGE 51)
Pearl Barley Tabbouleh (PAGE 136)
Fennel, Carrot, and Apple Slaw (PAGE 145)
Savory Pita Crisps (PAGE 66)

DRINKS
Red Bubbles Punch (PAGE 189)
Campari and Soda

swank cocktail party

There's a time in everyone's life for pulling out all the stops. It could be a milestone event like an engagement, or a yearly holiday party. For that posh feel, I always suggest a cocktail party with plenty of upscale hors d'oeuvres and a couple of signature cocktails (preferably at least one served in a fancy martini glass).

PASSED HORS D'OEUVRES

Seared Ahi on Wonton Crisps (PAGE 33)
Garlicky Beef Crostini with Caramelized Onion and Sage Whipped Cream
(PAGE 12)
Sliced Duck and Provençal Olive Tartine (PAGE 26)
Velvety Chicken Liver Mousse on Toast Points with Shallot Confit and
Tangerine Marmalade (PAGE 24)
Lemon Chive Blinis with Sour Cream and Salmon Roe (PAGE 35)

BUFFET HORS D'OEUVRES

Pissaladière (PAGE 60)
Smoked Salmon, Vodka, and Caviar Dip (PAGE 61)
Gorgonzola, Fig, and Pecan Cheese Terrine (PAGE 59)
Peppered Rosemary Oat Crackers (PAGE 67)

DRINKS

Rosemary Peach Cosmos (PAGE 177)
Absolute Apeach and Lemon Lime Soda

Sunday
* Make tangerine marmalade
  for chicken liver mousse
* Make shallot confit for chicken
  liver mousse

Monday
* Make gorgonzola terrine

Tuesday
* Make crostini for beef
* Make tartines
* Make oat crackers

Wednesday
* Make caramelized onion for
  beef crostini and onion mix
  for pissaladière
* Make wonton crisps

Thursday
* Make blinis and freeze
* Make chicken liver mousse
* Make smoked salmon
  vodka dip

Friday
* Make olive mix for
  duck tartine

Saturday
* Sear ahi
* Sear beef tenderloin
* Make sage whipped cream
* Sear duck breast
* Bake pissaladière

TIME LINE for Sunday Buffet

Friday
* Make blinis and freeze

Saturday
* Make stilton tart
* Make tabbouleh
* Bake cupcakes
* Make sugared rose petals

Sunday
* Make frittata
* Make pear waldorf
* Frost cupcakes

TIME LINE for Friday Dinner

Wednesday
* Make vinaigrette for salad
* Make blueberry cream for bread pudding

Thursday
* Make goat cheese torte
* Make cassoulet
* Roast brussels sprouts
* Make bread pudding

Friday
* Make chèvre toasts and assemble salad

brunch buffet

There are some people who wake up and can't look at food for a couple of hours (Steve), and there are some who wake up thinking about what to have for breakfast (me). I've always been a huge breakfast fan, and when I moved to New York City and discovered brunch—damn! I think it's the perfect way to entertain on a late Sunday morning.

BRUNCH BUFFET
Sweet Pea, Tarragon, and Chèvre Frittata (PAGE 125)
Stilton and Pear Tart (PAGE 54)
Lemon Chive Blinis with Sour Cream and Salmon Roe (PAGE 35)
Pearl Barley Tabbouleh (PAGE 136)
Pear Waldorf (PAGE 89)

DESSERT
Rosewater Cupcakes with Grenadine Frosting and Sugared Rose Petals (PAGE 164)

DRINKS
Pimm's Cup (PAGE 208)
Prosecco Mimosas

make-ahead dinner party

Whether you're a stay-at-home parent or a high-powered executive, you scramble to get through a never-ending list of projects and chores. It makes it hard to entertain, doesn't it? Here's a menu that can be mostly prepared one or two days in advance, leaving you virtually nothing to do on the day of.

HORS D'OEUVRES
Goat Cheese and Roasted Red Pepper Torte (PAGE 52)

FIRST COURSE
Baby Arugula Salad with Fig and Chèvre Toast (PAGE 83)

MAIN COURSE
Duck Sausage and White Bean Cassoulet (PAGE 112)
Caraway Roasted Brussels Sprouts (PAGE 138)

DESSERT
Lemon Brown Sugar Bread Pudding with Blueberry Cream (PAGE 159)

DRINKS
Aviation Cocktails, served with the tart (PAGE 175)
Red Wine: Australian Syrah

Elegant Vegetarian Dinner

Who said vegetarians have to settle for second best? That's a pet peeve of Jericho's, our executive catering chef. At many weddings, he feels that vegetarians are treated as an afterthought. They're short changed by being served extra-large helpings of rice pilaf and vegetables as their meal. Here's a menu that will satisfy not only your vegetarian friends, but also your meat lovers as well.

HORS D'OEUVRES
Mushroom Hazelnut Pâté (PAGE 65)

FIRST COURSE
Chilled Beets and Asparagus with Nasturtiums (PAGE 85)

MAIN COURSE
Three-Cheese Spaghetti Pie (PAGE 123)
Herb and Onion Flatbread (PAGE 149)

DESSERT
Raspberry Fool (PAGE 152)

DRINKS
Pomegranate Thyme Cordial (PAGE 197)
Red wine: Italian Sangiovese

Dessert Party

We'll throw dessert parties every once in a while on a weekend night when our friends don't have to get up early the next morning. We'll plan for 8 PM—that way everyone will have had a chance to eat dinner before arriving. We'll break out a board game and eat, drink, and laugh a lot. One important thing to keep in mind with this type of party is that you're feeding your guests sugar—a lot of it!. So make the portions small, two bites at most. That way, everyone feels comfortable taking one of each—or in my case, enough to slip me into a sugar coma.

Amaretto Profiteroles (PAGE 160)
Rosewater Cupcakes with Grenadine Frosting and Sugared Rose Petals (PAGE 164)
Steve's Espresso Shortbreads (PAGE 167)
Biscotti Regina (PAGE 169)

DRINKS
Thai Iced Coffee Punch (PAGE 190)
Black Muscat Dessert Wine

TIME LINE for Tuesday Dinner

Sunday
* Make mushroom pâté
* Make pomegranate thyme cordial

Monday
* Make spaghetti pie
* Make flatbread

Tuesday
* Make beet and asparagus salad
* Make raspberry fool

TIME LINE for Friday Party

Tuesday
* Make shortbread
* Make grenadine frosting for cupcakes

Wednesday
* Make biscotti

Thursday
* Bake profiteroles
* Make pastry cream for profiteroles
* Bake cupcakes
* Make sugared rose petals

Friday
* Assemble profiteroles
* Frost cupcakes

Liquor buying guide

Knowing how much liquor to buy isn't an exact science but there are some rules that can help you make informed choices. But like so many elements of hosting there will always be some unknowns. For your bar those unknowns range from the day's temperature to what I call the "lemming factor." The "lemming factor" is often set off by one party guest walking away from the bar with a pastel colored drink in a martini glass. The unsuspecting host then must look on in horror as the rest of the party lines up to ask for the pretty drink. Said pretty drink nearly always has a seldom requested main ingredient of which the mortified host has one lone bottle. Over the years we've learned to look for those little triggers (and I now get my butt over to the liquor store as soon as that first lemming hits the bar). But the unknown elements . . . let's just say that every now and then we're still thrown a curveball.

It was a lovely summer day, and we were catering a garden luncheon for a ladies' group. We had four tables of eight set with simple linen, starched napkins, and three-tier trays filled with mini scones and muffins. We set our bar up in a pristine corner of the garden with a backdrop of our hostess's daylilies and hydrangeas. We served traditional tea sandwiches, green salads, cold soup, and punches. One of the punches was alcoholic, and the other was not; both, however, were sweet.

What we didn't take into account, of course, was that we had all but set out a welcome mat for bees. They were thrilled to have the sweet juices and soft drinks so near their home and buzzed giddily about the bartender (a native Bostonian). None of us had any idea that he was patiently shooing the bees off his back and shoulders until he was finally stung. He let out a yelp and came racing past the guests, swatting at the air, and shouting, "I'm a *bahtendah*, not a beekeepah!"

I guess it's the curveballs that keep us swinging.

How do I know how much liquor to buy?	Without a doubt, this is hardest question I have to answer. There is no one simple equation. It's all muddied by factors, including time of day, time of year, gender, heritage and regional preferences, group dynamics, and, of course, menu choices. There are certainly tools that enable us to gauge how much liquor will be consumed, but as for the types of drinks that will be popular that day . . . well, it can be a bit of a crap shoot.
	So here are some basic tools you can use as a guide to your next liquor purchase. Keep these in mind—along with the aforementioned factors—and you will be in good shape.

How many drinks are there in a bottle?

For cocktails, highballs, and mixed drinks (based on a 1.5-ounce pour):

SPIRITS	DRINKS PER BOTTLE
750-milliliter bottle	16
1-liter bottle	22
1.75-liter bottle	39

For wine and champagne (based on a 5-ounce pour):

WINE AND CHAMPAGNE	DRINKS PER BOTTLE
750-milliliter bottle	5
1.5-liter bottle	10

What else do I need?	This is based on your average needs for mixers. If you're expecting to serve a lot of vodka and cranberry juice, for example, adjust these numbers.

MIXER	AMOUNT NEEDED
Soft drinks	One 2-liter bottle per 8 guests
Juices	One 2-liter bottle per 12 guests
Ice	1½–2 pounds per guest

How many bottles of wine should I buy for a dinner party?	You should allow one bottle of wine or champagne for every two or three guests. We always go through at least half a bottle of wine per guest at my dinner parties. But then again, our friends are all boozy.

WINE AND CHAMPAGNE	5 GUESTS	10 GUESTS	20 GUESTS
750-milliliter bottle	2+	4	8
1.5-liter bottle	1+	2	4

I'm having 25 guests for a cocktail party. Tell me what to buy!	Some people just don't want to do the math. This is a setup for a basic bar. It doesn't include liquors that aren't necessities—and it doesn't take into account the individual circumstances of the party or guests' personal preferences. This will get the average host through an average party. Bottle quantities, save for the standard 12-ounce size beer, are based on 750–milliliter size.

LIQUOR	BOTTLES NEEDED
Vodka	3
Gin	2
White Rum	1
Scotch	1
Bourbon	1
Dry Vermouth	1
White Wine	6
Red Wine	6
Beer	12

What other bar needs might I have?

We have an equipment checklist that must be pored over by two people before the supplies for any event are allowed to leave our kitchen. I recommend making one of your own . . . they're invaluable for making you feel organized and sane. Our basic bar list includes:

GARNISHES	MIXERS	BAR EQUIPMENT
Lemons	Cola	Beverage napkins
Limes	Diet cola	Wine opener
Large olives	Lemon-lime soda	Ice bucket
	Tonic	Church key can opener
	Club soda	Ice scoop
	Fresh lime juice	Cocktail shaker
	Orange juice	Liquor spouts
	Cranberry juice	Stir straws
	Bloody Mary mix	Sharp knife
	Sparkling water	Cutting board
	Ice	Bar towels
		Trash can
		Pitchers

What if I want to go all out?

Well, the sky's the limit on the top-shelf bar. If you're planning a large evening event, like an elegant reception or a wedding, you may want to consider adding from this list:

LIQUORS	AFTER-DINNER DRINKS	MIXERS AND GARNISHES
Champagne	Port	Pineapple juice
Tequila	Kahlua	Ginger ale
Dark rum	Grand Marnier	Milk or Cream
Triple sec	Amaretto	Cherries
Canadian whiskey	Sambuca	Stuffed olives
Single-malt Scotch	Frangelico	Bottled water
Campari	Brandy / Cognac	Angostura bitters
Sweet vermouth	Baileys Irish Cream	
Flavored liquors:		
(vodka, rum, schnapps)		

Why do you look nervous telling me all this?	Remember, I give you these lists with the following caveat: No one knows your guests better than you do. Adjust the amounts accordingly. If you know your guests to be heavy beer drinkers, stock more than the 12-pack I suggested! These are my best suggestions based on years of experience in the field. As caterers, we have the luxury of being able to bring backup supplies to avoid running low on something . . . of course, we also have to carry it.
What if I buy too much?	Throw another party! If you don't want to do that, remember that most liquor stores allow you to return unopened bottles, just check with your local purveyor for their policy. But it's always better to have leftover liquor than to run out of something your guests are enjoying. You wouldn't want to run out of Beef Bourguignon mid-dinner, would you? Either way, purchase brands you personally appreciate so you can enjoy them between parties.
What about those other considerations?	Here's more about the factors I touched on earlier . . . keep this in mind when planning. TIME OF DAY: Guests will drink less at a brunch open house than they will at an after-work soiree. PARTY THEME: Although both are Sunday afternoon events, guests will drink more at a Super Bowl party than at a baptism. LENGTH OF PARTY: Guests will start with about two drinks during the first hour of an event, then slow down to a drink and a half per hour thereafter. GEOGRAPHIC TASTES: Southerners drink much more bourbon than Northerners do. Think about where you live and how that affects the local palate. YOUR GUEST LIST: This is the most important factor to consider, and only you can answer this one. If we invite our friend Jerome and the softball team over, we'd better make sure we've got extra light beer in the fridge. If Dan's Italian family comes, we stock our bar with industrial-sized kegs of red wine. DRINK LIST: Are you planning to serve any special cocktails? For example, one person having a rosy cosmopolitan at a house party invariably causes a rush to the bar. Unless the host is prepared, she will run out of cranberry juice.

Can I have just one more of those cute charts?	Here are some tips that should help the wine-aphobes approach wine pairing with "claret-y." Over the years, wines have developed a large spectrum of subtleties within each varietal. What this means is that "white wine with fish" no longer applies as a hard and fast rule. There are really two aspects on which to focus your wine pairing nowadays: the weight or intensity of the food, and the preparation or sauce of the dish. Just don't ever forget the wine rule that trumps all others: drink what you like!

"Match weight of wine with food." The weight of a wine, whether light-, medium- or full-bodied should generally match the weight and intensity of the dish.

FOOD	FLAVORS	WINE SUGGESTION	QUALITIES
Leek and Cremini Ravioli with Red and Yellow Tomato Concassé	Delicate, meaty, sweet, light	Riesling	Light and versatile. Acidic enough to balance the sweetness of the sauce, yet weighty enough to match the mushrooms.
Chicken, Sausage, and Shrimp Stew	Varied in texture and flavors with fennel, orange, thyme	Rioja	Smack in the middle of the red wine spectrum. Will not overpower the delicate aspects, yet can stand up to the sausage.
Beef and Veal Stifado	Sturdy Greek; feta, rosemary, cinnamon	Syrah, Shiraz	Hearty stew needs hearty wine, so pull out the stops.

"Match wine to sauce rather than the meat/fish it comes on." Wine should complement the most prominent feature of the dish. That flavor often comes from the preparation.

FOOD	FLAVORS	WINE SUGGESTION	QUALITIES
Pan-Fried Soft-Shell Crabs	Fried preparation, creamy buttermilk	Champagne	Light enough for the delicate crabs and yet will clean up the palate from the heavy fried-ness.
Balsamic Mushroom Chicken Breast	Slightly sweet, woodsy, tangy sauce	Dolcetto, Barbera	Lighter reds with softer tannins and some complexity.
Duck Sausage and White Bean Cassoulet	Savory, concentrated, herby, earthy	Rhone, preferably southern	Robust, bit of spice and gripping tannins. This French wine is a perfect match to a French Cassoulet.

acknowledgments

Great thanks go to Leslie Stoker, Ann Treistman, Marisa Bulzone, and all the good folks at Stewart, Tabori & Chang for their excitement and guidance, and to Dorian Karchmar and Jason Hodes at William Morris. Thanks to Food Network for giving us such a strong platform to spread our entertaining vision and to all the great people there, from our *Party Line* crew to the production offices . . . and a special shout out to the team from *The Next Food Network Star* and to the other finalists, all of whom have special places in our hearts.

On the creative side, thanks to Laurie for being so talented and exacting and to her team, Josephine and Chad. Kudos to Susi for putting together a book that looks exactly the way we wanted it to. We must mention Joanna Pulcini for knowing that we had a book in us before we did and for introducing us to Lee Butala, the first guy we go to with questions and a guy we're pleased to call our friend; Lee, you had tremendous impact in shaping this book. Ellen Malloy gets credit for just telling us where to be at what time and for being a surprise sommelier, as does our staff at Hearty Boys for keeping the business running while we tried to meet deadlines, shoot TV shows, and keep the baby fed, especially Christine and Jericho, who, when confronted with a brick wall built a door. Thanks to all our friends who got recruited for this book, whether they came to our photo shoot parties (as if the free food and full bar wasn't thanks enough), helped with testing recipes (the liquor chapter being particularly taxing), or just put in their two cents (Donna, here's your name.)

Thanks to Andrea for being such an incredible caretaker to Nate while we are at the computers and thanks to Nate for being the most patient, sturdy little guy anyone could ever love. Thanks to Jim and Vicki from the start, and to Francine for the knowledge.

And a final thank you to the original Hearty Boys. We can't write the stories in this book without remembering the warm summer nights in the backyard on Halsted, kicking back under the little Christmas lights we had in the trees, drinking beers from the reach in after getting back from parties. We wouldn't be here without you.

CONVERSION CHART

WEIGHT EQUIVALENTS

The metric weights given in this chart are not exact equivalents, but have been rounded up or down slightly to make measuring easier.

AVOIRDUPOIS	METRIC
¼ oz	7 g
½ oz	15 g
1 oz	30 g
2 oz	60 g
3 oz	90 g
4 oz	115 g
5 oz	150 g
6 oz	175 g
7 oz	200 g
8 oz (½ lb)	225 g
9 oz	250 g
10 oz	300 g
11 oz	325 g
12 oz	350 g
13 oz	375 g
14 oz	400 g
15 oz	425 g
16 oz (1 lb)	450 g
1½ lb	750 g
2 lb	900 g
2¼ lb	1 kg
3 lb	1.4 kg
4 lb	1.8 kg

VOLUME EQUIVALENTS

These are not exact equivalents for American cups and spoons, but have been rounded up or down slightly to make measuring easier.

AMERICAN	METRIC	IMPERIAL
¼ teaspoon	1.2 ml	
½ teaspoon	2.5 ml	
1 teaspoon	5.0 ml	
½ T (1.5 teaspoons)	7.5 ml	
1 T (3 teaspoons)	15 ml	
¼ cup (4 T)	60 ml	2 fl oz
⅓ cup (5 T)	75 ml	2.5 fl oz
½ cup (8 T)	125 ml	4 fl oz
½ cup (10 T)	150 ml	5 fl oz
¾ cup (12 T)	175 ml	6 fl oz
1 cup (16 T)	250 ml	8 fl oz
1¼ cups	300 ml	10 fl oz (H pt)
1½ cups	350 ml	12 fl oz
2 cups (1 pint)	500 ml	16 fl oz
2½ cups	625 ml	20 fl oz (1 pint)
1 quart	1 liter	32 fl oz

OVEN TEMPERATURE EQUIVALENTS

OVEN MARK	F	C	GAS
Very cool	250–275	130–140	½–1
Cool	300	150	2
Warm	325	170	3
Moderate	350	180	4
Moderately hot	375	190	5
	400	200	6
Hot	425	220	7
	450	230	8
Very hot	475	250	9

index

A

Ahi, seared, on wonton crisps, *32, 33*
Ale, in lemon shandy, 174
Almond punch, 188, *188*
Amaretto:
  butternut scotch, 198
  financier, 199
  profiteroles, 160–61, *161*
Angel's tit, *171,* 194
Anise roasted green beans, 139
Appetizers. *See* Dips; Hors
  d'oeuvres; Salads; Soups;
  Starters
Apple:
  fennel, and carrot slaw,
  144, 145
  jam, 16, *17*
  picker's punch, 184
  ruby, 190, *191*
  tart, rustic, 162, *163*
Apricot(s):
  cider-braised pork roast
  stuffed with figs and, *98, 99*
  punch with basil floats,
  193, 193
  wrapped in bacon,
  glazed, 20
Artichoke:
  fritters, 36, *37*
  soda, 199
  spinach, and bacon dip, 55
Arugula, baby, salad with figs
  and chèvre toast, *5,* 83
Ashtrays, emptying, 169
Asparagus and beets, chilled,
  with nasturtiums, *84, 85*
Averna, in digestivo, 199
Aviation cocktail, 175

B

Bacon:
  and blue cheese "Matt loaf,"
  104

glazed apricots wrapped in,
  20
lamb-stuffed dates wrapped
  in, 21
spinach, and artichoke dip, 55
Balsamic (vinegar):
  honey glaze, 20
  mushroom chicken breast,
  108, 109
  pear rosemary, 47
Bananas foster with chocolate
  crème fraîche pot, 154, *155*
Barley, pearl, tabbouleh, 136, *137*
Bar setups, 190
Basil floats, 193, *193*
Bathroom beautification, 131
Beef:
  bacon and blue cheese "Matt
  loaf," 104
  braised short ribs with
  Merlot reduction, 100
  garlicky, crostini with
  caramelized onion and
  sage whipped cream, 12–13
  kebabs, Middle Eastern,
  102, *103*
  and veal stifado, 101
Beer, 177, 181
  lemon shandy, 174
Beets and asparagus, chilled,
  with nasturtiums, *84, 85*
Berries, maple, cardamom
  shortcake with, 153
Biscotti regina, 169
Biscuit topping, 107
Blackened pork chop with
  smoked oyster stuffing,
  94, *95*
Black sangria, 192
Blinis, lemon chive, with sour
  cream and salmon roe, 35
Blueberry cream, 159
Blue cheese. *See also* Gorgonzola
  and bacon "Matt loaf," 104

and caramelized onion dip, 62
Stilton and pear tart, 54
Blush sangria, 192
Boule, rosemary Gorgonzola
  mushrooms in, 56, *57*
Brandy:
  the diablo, 198
  nutty Alexander, 198
Bread(s). *See also* Crostini
  chèvre toast, *5,* 83
  croutons, 86
  herb and onion flatbread, 149
  Moroccan olive flatbread, 148
  pudding, lemon brown
  sugar, with blueberry
  cream, *158, 159*
  tomatillo Cheddar corn-
  bread, 147
Brussels sprouts, caraway
  roasted, 138
Butter(s), 147
  orange, 34
  orange tarragon, 110
  tarragon, sauce, 93
Butternut scotch, 198

C

Caesar salad, hearts of
  romaine, 86
Cajun:
  crab-stuffed pepperoncini, 38
  crawfish étouffée, *118,* 119
  seasoning mix, 119
Calvados, in ruby apple, 190, *191*
Campari:
  apricot punch with basil
  floats, *193, 193*
  the diablo, 198
  red bubbles, 189
Candied orange zest, 195, *195*
Candles, 122, 138
Caprese cups, 31
Caraway roasted Brussels
  sprouts, 138

Cardamom shortcake with
  maple berries, 153
Carrot, fennel, and apple slaw,
  144, 145
Cassoulet, duck sausage and
  white bean, 112–13, *113*
Catfish, cured, in vuelve la vida,
  50, 51
Cauliflower Cheddar gratin, 142
Caviar:
  smoked salmon, and vodka
  dip, *45,* 61
  -stuffed eggs, *76, 77*
Centerpieces, 130
Chair arrangements, 89
Champagne, 211, 212
  French 75, 173
  opening, 188
  red bubbles, 189
Cheddar:
  cauliflower gratin, 142
  shortbread, shaved ham on,
  with apple jam, 16, *17*
  tomatillo cornbread, 147
Cheese, 69. *See also specific cheeses*
  three-, spaghetti pie, 123
Chesapeake tartar sauce, 115
Chèvre. *See* Goat cheese
Chicken:
  breast, balsamic mushroom,
  108, 109
  breast with orange tarragon
  butter, French, *2,* 110
  grilled, white bean, and basil
  chili, 111
  pot pie, 106–7, *107*
  red curry, wontons with plum
  sauce, *22, 23*
  satay, sesame, 28
  sausage, and shrimp stew, 105
Chicken liver mousse on rye
  with shallot confit and
  tangerine marmalade,
  24–25

Chickpeas, in rosemary-scented hummus, 63
Chili, grilled chicken, white bean, and basil, 111
Chocolate:
    cream cheese cupcakes, 166, 167
    crème fraîche pot, bananas foster with, 154, 155
    espresso with candied orange peel, 195, 195
    white, risotto with orange ganache, 156–57, 157
Cider-braised pork roast stuffed with figs and apricots, 98, 99
Cocktails. See Libations; Punches
Coffee, 157, 168
    chocolate espresso with candied orange peel, 195, 195
    espresso shortbreads, 168
    sunny Irishman, 194
    Thai iced, punch, 190
Concassé, red and yellow tomato, 73
Condiments. See also Butter(s); Cream; Dressings; Sauces
    apple jam, 16, 17
    candied orange zest, 195, 195
    caramelized onion, 13
    gremolata, 117
    harissa yogurt, 80
    honey balsamic glaze, 20
    shallot confit, 25
    sugared rose petals, 165
    tangerine marmalade, 25
Cookies, sesame seed, 169
Coriander lime shrimp with mango skewers, 29
Cornbread, tomatillo Cheddar, 147
Cornmeal peppercorn crust, 52
Cosmopolitan, rosemary peach, 176, 177
Coulis, red pepper, 87
Couscous, fig and rosemary, 134
Crab(meat)(s):
    soft-shell, pan-fried, with Chesapeake tartar sauce, 114–15

-stuffed pepperoncini, Cajun, 38
    vuelve la vida, 50, 51
Crackers, peppered rosemary oat, 67
Crawfish étouffée, Cajun, 118, 119
Cream:
    amaretto, 161
    blueberry, 159
    Dijon whipped, 121
    raspberry fool, 152
    roasted tomato, 19
    sage whipped, 13
Cream cheese frosting, 166, 167
Crème de cacao, in nutty Alexander, 198
Crème de cassis:
    el diablo punch, 186, 187
    digestivo, 199
Cremini and leek ravioli with red and yellow tomato concassé, 71, 72–73
Croque monsieur, petit, 15
Crostini:
    basic, with variations, 68
    garlicky beef, with caramelized onion and sage whipped cream, 12–13
Croutons, 86
Crusts, 54, 146
    cornmeal peppercorn, 52
Cuba libre, real, 173
Cucumber yogurt sauce, 102
Cupcakes:
    chocolate cream cheese, 166, 167
    rosewater, with grenadine frosting and sugared rose petals, 151, 164–65
Curaçao:
    the diablo, 198
    ruby apple, 190, 191
Curry, red, chicken wontons with plum sauce, 22, 23
Cynar, in artichoke soda, 199

D

Dates, lamb-stuffed, wrapped in bacon, 21

Desserts, 150–69
    amaretto profiteroles, 160–61, 161
    apple tart, rustic, 162, 163
    bananas foster with chocolate crème fraîche pot, 154, 155
    biscotti regina (sesame seed cookies), 169
    cardamom shortcake with maple berries, 153
    chocolate cream cheese cupcakes, 166, 167
    espresso shortbreads, 168
    lemon brown sugar bread pudding with blueberry cream, 158, 159
    raspberry fool, 152
    rosewater cupcakes with grenadine frosting and sugared rose petals, 151, 164–65
    white chocolate risotto with orange ganache, 156–57, 157
Diablo, the, 198
Diablo punch, el, 186, 187
Digestivo, 199
Dijon whipped cream, 121
Dips:
    blue cheese and caramelized onion, 62
    rosemary-scented hummus, 63
    savory pita crisps for, 66
    smoked salmon, vodka, and caviar, 45, 61
    spinach, artichoke, and bacon, 55
Dollar Stores, 115
Dressings:
    Caesar, 86
    grape vinaigrette, 82
    green goddess, 87
    vinaigrette, 83
Drinks. See Libations; Punches
Duck:
    sausage and white bean cassoulet, 112–13, 113
    sliced, and Provençal olive tartine, 26, 27

E

Eggs:
    caviar-stuffed, 76, 77
    sweet pea, tarragon, and chèvre frittata, 124, 125
Espresso:
    chocolate, with candied orange peel, 195, 195
    shortbreads, 168

F

Falafel in lettuce cups with garlic tahini sauce, 42, 43
Fennel, carrot, and apple slaw, 144, 145
Feta, simple salad with grape vinaigrette, walnuts and, 82
Fig(s):
    baby arugula salad with chèvre toast and, 5, 83
    cider-braised pork roast stuffed with apricots and, 98, 99
    Gorgonzola, and pecan cheese terrine, 58, 59
    and rosemary couscous, 134
    wine-soaked, and goat cheese, 46
Financier, 199
Flatbreads:
    herb and onion, 149
    Moroccan olive, 148
Floridita, la, 182
Flower arrangements, 141
Fool, raspberry, 152
French 75 (cocktail), 173
French chicken breast with orange tarragon butter, 2, 110
Frittata, sweet pea, tarragon, and chèvre, 124, 125
Fritters, artichoke, 36, 37
Frostings:
    cream cheese, 166, 167
    grenadine, 165

G

Ganache, orange, 157
Garlic(ky):
    beef crostini with caramelized onion and sage whipped cream, 12–13

Parmesan crostini, 68
tahini sauce, 42
Gazpacho, watermelon,
　　shooters, *40, 41*
Gin:
　　aviation cocktail, 175
　　French 75, 173
　　Pegu club, 181, *181*
　　the vesper, 172
Ginger beer, in Moscow mule,
　　182, *183*
Gingered lemonade, 174
Glassware, 197
Goat cheese:
　　chèvre toast, *5, 83*
　　and roasted red pepper
　　　torte, 52
　　sweet pea, tarragon, and
　　　chèvre frittata, *124, 125*
　　wine-soaked figs and, 46
Goccia di limone, 172
Gorgonzola:
　　fig, and pecan cheese terrine,
　　　58, 59
　　herb braised Bosc pears with
　　　frizzled prosciutto and,
　　　88–89
　　rosemary mushrooms in
　　　boule, 56, *57*
Grape vinaigrette, 82
Green beans, anise roasted, 139
Green goddess dressing, 87
Gremolata, 117
Grenadine frosting, 165
Grilled:
　　chicken, white bean, and
　　　basil chili, 111
　　Middle Eastern beef kebabs,
　　　102, *103*
Grits, in herbed porridge, 132
Gruyère cheese, in petit croque
　　monsieur, 15
Guinness float, 200, *201*

H

Ham:
　　petit croque monsieur, 15
　　shaved, on Cheddar
　　　shortbread with apple
　　　jam, 16, *17*
Harissa yogurt, 80

Hazelnut:
　　liqueur, in nutty Alexander,
　　　198
　　mushroom pâté, *64, 65*
Hearts of romaine Caesar
　　salad, 86
Herb(ed):
　　crostini, 68
　　and onion flatbread, 149
　　porridge, 132
Hibiscus margarita, 178, *179*
Honey:
　　balsamic glaze, 20
　　lemon tea punch, 184
　　roasted parsnip bisque, 79
Hors d'oeuvres, buffet, 44–69.
　　See also Dips
　　crostini with variations, 68
　　goat cheese and roasted red
　　　pepper torte, 52
　　Gorgonzola, fig, and pecan
　　　cheese terrine, *58, 59*
　　mozzarella with basil and
　　　crushed red pepper, 48, *49*
　　mushroom hazelnut pâté,
　　　64, 65
　　nuts, spiced cocktail, 69
　　peppered rosemary oat
　　　crackers, 67
　　pissaladière, 60
　　pita crisps, savory, 66
　　ricotta salata with freshly
　　　sliced pears and pear bal-
　　　samic vinegar, 47
　　rosemary Gorgonzola mush-
　　　rooms in boule, 56, *57*
　　Stilton and pear tart, 54
　　three-mushroom tart, 53
　　vuelve la vida, *50, 51*
　　wine-soaked figs and goat
　　　cheese, 46
Hors d'oeuvres, passed, 10–42
　　ahi, seared, on wonton
　　　crisps, *32, 33*
　　apricots wrapped in bacon,
　　　glazed, 20
　　artichoke fritters, *36, 37*
　　beef crostini with caramelized
　　　onion and sage whipped
　　　cream, 12–13
　　Caprese cups, 31

chicken liver mousse on
　　rye with shallot confit and
　　tangerine marmalade,
　　24–25
coriander lime shrimp with
　　mango skewers, 29
crab-stuffed pepperoncini,
　　Cajun, 38
duck, sliced, and Provençal
　　olive tartine, 26, *27*
falafel in lettuce cups with
　　garlic tahini sauce, 42, *43*
ham, shaved, on Cheddar
　　shortbread with apple
　　jam, 16, *17*
lamb-stuffed dates wrapped
　　in bacon, 21
lemon chive blinis with sour
　　cream and salmon roe, 35
petit croque monsieur, 15
pork braciola, skewered,
　　with roasted tomato
　　cream, 18–19, *19*
red curry chicken wontons
　　with plum sauce, *22, 23*
sesame chicken satay, 28
shrimp tonnato, 30
smoked salmon canapés
　　with orange butter and
　　capers, 34
spinach Parmesan balls, 39
watermelon gazpacho
　　shooters, *40, 41*
Hummus, rosemary-scented, 63

I

Ice, 41, 180, 187
Iceberg wedge with green
　　goddess dressing, 87
Irish pirate, 194

K

Kebabs, Middle Eastern beef,
　　102, *103*

L

Lager, in lemon shandy, 174
Lamb:
　　pepper-encrusted rack of,
　　　with Madagascar green
　　　peppercorn sauce, 96–97

-stuffed dates wrapped in
　　bacon, 21
Leek(s):
　　braised, with sel de mer, 139
　　and cremini ravioli with
　　　red and yellow tomato
　　　concassé, *71, 72–73*
Lemon:
　　brown sugar bread pudding
　　　with blueberry cream,
　　　158, 159
　　chive blinis with sour cream
　　　and salmon roe, 35
　　dipping sauce, 36
　　goccia di limone, 172
　　honey tea punch, 184
　　shandy, 174
Lemonade, gingered, 174
Lentil soup, Moroccan, with
　　harissa yogurt, 80
Libations, 170–200. *See also*
　　Punches
　　angel's tit, *171,* 194
　　artichoke soda, 199
　　aviation cocktail, 175
　　butternut scotch, 198
　　chocolate espresso with
　　　candied orange peel,
　　　195, *195*
　　the diablo, 198
　　digestivo, 199
　　financier, 199
　　la Floridita, 182
　　French 75, 173
　　goccia di limone, 172
　　Guinness float, 200, *201*
　　hibiscus margarita, 178, *179*
　　Irish pirate, 194
　　lemon shandy, 174
　　Moscow mule, 182, *183*
　　nutty Alexander, 198
　　Pegu club, 181, *181*
　　Pimm's cup, 180, *180*
　　pomegranate sour, 173
　　pomegranate thyme cordial,
　　　196, 197
　　real Cuba libre, 173
　　rosemary peach
　　　cosmopolitan, *176, 177*
　　sunny Irishman, 194
　　the vesper, 172

Lighting, 138
Lillet blanc, in the vesper, 172
Lingonberry-stuffed meatballs
  with tarragon butter
  sauce, 91, 92–93
Liquor. See also Libations
  buying guide, 210–15
  cost of, 177
Lobster, in seafood Newburg
  with gremolata, 116–17,
  117

M
Madagascar green peppercorn
  sauce, 97
Mahogany rice pilaf, 135
Main dishes, 90–125
  bacon and blue cheese "Matt
  loaf," 104
  beef and veal stifado, 101
  beef kebabs, Middle Eastern,
  102, 103
  chicken, grilled, white bean,
  and basil chili, 111
  chicken, sausage, and shrimp
  stew, 105
  chicken breast, balsamic
  mushroom, 108, 109
  chicken breast with orange
  tarragon butter, French,
  2, 110
  chicken pot pie, 106–7, 107
  crawfish étouffée, Cajun,
  118, 119
  duck sausage and white bean
  cassoulet, 112–13, 113
  lamb, pepper-encrusted rack
  of, with Madagascar
  green peppercorn sauce,
  96–97
  meatballs, lingonberry-
  stuffed, with tarragon
  butter sauce, 91, 92–93
  pork chop, blackened, with
  smoked oyster stuffing,
  94, 95
  pork roast, cider-braised,
  stuffed with figs and apricots, 98, 99
  rotini, baked, with tomato
  cream, 122

salmon Wellington, 120–21,
  121
seafood Newburg with gre-
  molata, 116–17, 117
short ribs, braised, with
  Merlot reduction, 100
soft-shell crabs, pan-fried,
  with Chesapeake tartar
  sauce, 114–15
sweet pea, tarragon, and
  chèvre frittata, 124, 125
three-cheese spaghetti pie,
  123
Mango, coriander lime shrimp
  skewers with, 29
Maple berries, cardamom
  shortcake with, 153
Maraschino liqueur:
  angel's tit, 171, 194
  aviation cocktail, 175
Margarita, hibiscus, 178, 179
Marmalade, tangerine, 25
Martini, vesper, 172
Meatballs, lingonberry-stuffed,
  with tarragon butter
  sauce, 91, 92–93
Menu planning, 21, 28, 135, 140
Menus, 202–9
  Afternoon Garden Party, 206
  An Italian-Inspired Buffet
  Dinner, 204
  Brunch Buffet, 208
  Comfort Food with Friends,
  204
  Dessert Party, 209
  Elegant Vegetarian Dinner,
  209
  Make-Ahead Dinner Party, 208
  Pre-Event Cocktails, 206
  A Seated Dinner Party, 205
  Sports Sunday, 205
  Swank Cocktail Party, 207
Merlot reduction, braised short
  ribs with, 100
Middle Eastern beef kebabs,
  102, 103
Moroccan:
  lentil soup with harissa
  yogurt, 80
  olive flatbread, 148
Moscow mule, 182, 183

Mozzarella:
  Caprese cups, 31
  fresh, with basil and crushed
  red pepper, 48, 49
Mushroom(s):
  balsamic chicken breast,
  108, 109
  cremini and leek ravioli with
  red and yellow tomato
  concassé, 71, 72–73
  hazelnut pâté, 64, 65
  rosemary Gorgonzola, in
  boule, 56, 57
  three-, tart, 53
Music, 143

N
Napkins, 31, 112
Nasturtiums, chilled beets
  and asparagus with,
  84, 85
Nuts, spiced cocktail, 69
Nutty Alexander, 198

O
Oat crackers, peppered
  rosemary, 67
Old Bay and lemon roasted
  potatoes, 131
Olive:
  flatbread, Moroccan, 148
  Provençal, and sliced duck
  tartine, 26, 27
Onion(s):
  caramelized, 13
  caramelized, and blue cheese
  dip, 62
  and herb flatbread, 149
  pie, rustic, 146
  pissaladière, 60
Open houses, 136
Orange:
  butter, 34
  ganache, 157
  liqueur, in Pegu club,
  181, 181
  liqueur, in sunny Irishman,
  194
  tarragon butter, 110
  zest, candied, 195, 195
Outdoor parties, 61

Oyster, smoked:
  polenta, 74, 75
  stuffing, blackened pork
  chop with, 94, 95

P
Parmesan:
  garlic crostini, 68
  spinach balls, 39
Parsnip, honey roasted,
  bisque, 79
Pasta:
  baked rotini with tomato
  cream, 122
  leek and cremini ravioli with
  red and yellow tomato
  concassé, 71, 72–73
  three-cheese spaghetti pie,
  123
Pastry cream, amaretto, 161
Pâté, mushroom hazelnut, 64, 65
Pâte sucrée, 162
Pea, sweet:
  tarragon, and chèvre frittata,
  124, 125
  and tarragon puree, 134
Peach rosemary cosmopolitan,
  176, 177
Pear(s):
  eau de vie, in financier, 199
  freshly sliced, ricotta salata
  with, and pear balsamic
  vinegar, 47
  herb braised Bosc, with
  Gorgonzola and frizzled
  prosciutto, 88–89
  and Stilton tart, 54
  Waldorf, 89
Pearl barley tabbouleh, 136, 137
Pecan, Gorgonzola, and fig
  cheese terrine, 58, 59
Pegu club, 181, 181
Pepper(corn)(ed):
  cornmeal crust, 52
  -encrusted rack of lamb
  with Madagascar green
  peppercorn sauce, 96–97
  rosemary oat crackers, 67
Pepper, red. See Red bell pepper
Pepperoncini, Cajun crab-
  stuffed, 38

Petit croque monsieur, 15
Pies:
    chicken pot, 106–7, *107*
    onion, rustic, 146
    three-cheese spaghetti, 123
Pimm's cup, 180, *180*
Piña colada punch, 189
Pissaladière, 60
Pita crisps, savory, 66
Polenta, smoked oyster, 74, *75*
Pomegranate:
    sour, 173
    thyme cordial, *196, 197*
Ponche almendrado, 188, *188*
Pork:
    braciola, skewered, with
        roasted tomato cream,
        18–19, *19*
    chop, blackened, with
        smoked oyster stuffing,
        94, *95*
    roast, cider-braised, stuffed
        with figs and apricots,
        98, *99*
Porridge, herbed, 132
Potato(es):
    fingerling, hash, 130
    Old Bay and lemon roasted,
        131
    truffled mashed, 129
    Yukon gold, oven-roasted, 128
Pot pie, chicken, 106–7, *107*
Pouring drinks, 200
Presentation tips, 15, 63, 129
Profiteroles, amaretto,
    160–61, *161*
Prosciutto, frizzled, herb
    braised Bosc pears
    with Gorgonzola and,
    88–89
Prosecco:
    apricot punch with basil
        floats, 193, *193*
    French 75, 173
    ruby apple, 190, *191*
Punches, 185
    almond (ponche
        almendrado), 188, *188*
    apple picker's, 184
    apricot, with basil floats,
        193, 193

black sangria, 192
blush sangria, 192
el diablo, *186, 187*
honey lemon tea, 184
iced coffee, Thai, 190
piña colada, 189
red bubbles, 189
ruby apple, 190, *191*
rum refresher, 187
wicked tea, 185, *185*

R
Raspberry fool, 152
Ravioli, leek and cremini, with
    red and yellow tomato
    concassé, *71, 72–73*
Real Cuba libre, 173
Red bell pepper:
    coulis, 87
    roasted, and goat cheese
        torte, 52
Red bubbles, 189
Red curry chicken wontons
    with plum sauce, *22, 23*
Rice. *See also* Risotto
    herbed porridge, 132
    mahogany, pilaf, 135
Ricotta salata with freshly
    sliced pears and pear
    balsamic vinegar, 47
Risotto:
    saffron, cakes, 133
    white chocolate, with
        orange ganache, 156–57,
        157
Romaine, hearts of, Caesar
    salad, 86
Romas, roasted, 74
Root vegetables, oven-roasted,
    141
Rosemary:
    Gorgonzola mushrooms in
        boule, 56, *57*
    peach cosmopolitan, *176,* 177
    pear balsamic vinegar, 47
    peppered oat crackers, 67
    -scented hummus, 63
Rosewater cupcakes with
    grenadine frosting and
    sugared rose petals, *151,*
    164–65

Rotini, baked, with tomato
    cream, 122
Ruby apple, 190, *191*
Rum:
    apple picker's punch, 184
    la Floridita, 182
    Irish pirate, 194
    piña colada punch, 189
    real Cuba libre, 173
    refresher, 187
    Thai iced coffee punch, 190
    wicked tea, 185, *185*
Rustic apple tart, 162, *163*
Rustic onion pie, 146

S
Saffron risotto cakes, 133
Sage whipped cream, 13
Salads:
    baby arugula, with figs and
        chèvre toast, *5,* 83
    fennel, carrot, and apple
        slaw, *144,* 145
    hearts of romaine Caesar, 86
    iceberg wedge with green
        goddess dressing, 87
    pear Waldorf, 89
    simple, with grape
        vinaigrette, feta, and
        walnuts, 82
Salmon:
    smoked, canapés with orange
        butter and capers, 34
    smoked, vodka, and caviar
        dip, *45,* 61
    Wellington, 120–21, *121*
Salmon roe, lemon chive blinis
    with sour cream and, 35
Sangria:
    black, 192
    blush, 192
Satay, sesame chicken, 28
Sauces. *See also* Butter(s);
    Cream; Dressings
    cucumber yogurt, 102
    garlic tahini, 42
    lemon dipping, 36
    Madagascar green
        peppercorn, 97
    pear rosemary balsamic
        vinegar, 47

red and yellow tomato con-
    cassé, 73
red pepper coulis, 87
tarragon butter, 93
tartar, Chesapeake, 115
Sausage:
    chicken, and shrimp stew,
        105
    duck, and white bean
        cassoulet, 112–13, *113*
Scallops:
    seafood Newburg with
        gremolata, 116–17, *117*
    vuelve la vida, *50,* 51
Scotch, butternut, 198
Seafood Newburg with gremo-
    lata, 116–17, *117*
Sesame (seed):
    chicken satay, 28
    cookies (biscotti regina), 169
Shallot confit, 25
Shandy, lemon, 174
Shortbreads:
    Cheddar, shaved ham on,
        with apple jam, 16, *17*
    espresso, 168
Shortcake, cardamom, with
    maple berries, 153
Short ribs, braised, with Merlot
    reduction, 100
Shrimp:
    chicken, and sausage stew,
        105
    coriander lime, with mango
        skewers, 29
    seafood Newburg with
        gremolata, 116–17, *117*
    tonnato, 30
    vuelve la vida, *50,* 51
Side dishes, 126–49. *See also*
    Potato(es)
    Brussels sprouts, caraway
        roasted, 138
    cauliflower Cheddar gratin,
        142
    cornbread, tomatillo
        Cheddar, 147
    couscous, fig and rosemary,
        134
    fennel, carrot, and apple
        slaw, *144,* 145

green beans, anise roasted, 139

herb and onion flatbread, 149

herbed porridge, 132

leeks, braised, with sel de mer, 139

mahogany rice pilaf, 135

olive flatbread, Moroccan, 148

onion pie, rustic, 146

pearl barley tabbouleh, 136, *137*

root vegetables, oven-roasted, 141

saffron risotto cakes, 133

tarragon and sweet pea puree, 134

vegetable confetti, pan-sautéed, 140

Skewers, 18

coriander lime shrimp with mango, 29

Middle Eastern beef kebabs, 102, *103*

pork braciola with roasted tomato cream, 18–19, *19*

sesame chicken satay, 28

Slaw, fennel, carrot, and apple, *144*, 145

Soft-shell crabs, pan-fried, with Chesapeake tartar sauce, 114–15

Soups:

honey roasted parsnip bisque, 79

lentil, Moroccan, with harissa yogurt, 80

stracciatella, 78

watermelon gazpacho shooters, *40*, 41

Spaghetti pie, three-cheese, 123

Spiced cocktail nuts, 69

Spinach:

artichoke, and bacon dip, 55

Parmesan balls, 39

Squid, in vuelve la vida, *50*, 51

Staff, hiring, 14

Starters, 70–89. *See also* Dips; Hors d'oeuvres; Salads; Soups

beets and asparagus, chilled, with nasturtiums, *84*, 85

caviar-stuffed eggs, *76*, *77*

herb braised Bosc pears with Gorgonzola and frizzled prosciutto, 88–89

leek and cremini ravioli with red and yellow tomato concassé, *71*, *72–73*

smoked oyster polenta, 74, *75*

Stifado, beef and veal, 101

Stilton and pear tart, 54

Stout, in Guinness float, 200, *201*

Stracciatella, 78

Strawberries, in cardamom shortcake with maple berries, 153

Sunny Irishman, 194

Swiss chard, sautéed, 73

T

Tabbouleh, pearl barley, 136, *137*

Tablecloths, 48

Tahini sauce, garlic, 42

Tangerine marmalade, 25

Tarragon:

butter sauce, *91*, *92–93*, 93

orange butter, 110

sweet pea, and chèvre frittata, *124*, 125

and sweet pea puree, 134

Tartar sauce, Chesapeake, 115

Tartine, sliced duck and Provençal olive, 26, *27*

Tarts, 55

apple, rustic, 162, *163*

pissaladière, 60

Stilton and pear, 54

three-mushroom, 53

Tea:

almond punch, 188, *188*

apple picker's punch, 184

hibiscus, 178

honey lemon, punch, 184

rum refresher, 187

wicked, 185, *185*

Tequila:

almond punch, 188, *188*

el diablo punch, *186*, 187

hibiscus margarita, 178, *179*

Terrine, Gorgonzola, fig, and pecan cheese, *58*, *59*

Thai iced coffee punch, 190

Theme parties, 81

Three-cheese spaghetti pie, 123

Three-mushroom tart, 53

Thyme pomegranate cordial, *196*, 197

Tomatillo Cheddar cornbread, 147

Tomato(es):

Caprese cups, 31

cream, baked rotini with, 122

red and yellow, concassé, 73

roasted, cream, 19

Romas, roasted, 74

Torte, goat cheese and roasted red pepper, 52

Trash receptacles, 18, 62

Truffled mashed potatoes, 129

Tuna:

seared ahi on wonton crisps, *32*, *33*

shrimp tonnato, 30

V

Veal and beef stifado, 101

Vegetable confetti, pan-sautéed, 140

Vesper, the, 172

Vinaigrettes, 83

grape, 82

Vodka, 177

goccia di limone, 172

honey lemon tea punch, 184

Moscow mule, 182, *183*

pomegranate thyme cordial, *196*, 197

rosemary peach cosmopolitan, *176*, 177

smoked salmon, and caviar dip, *45*, 61

Thai iced coffee punch, 190

the vesper, 172

Vuelve la vida, *50*, 51

W

Waldorf, pear, 89

Water, pouring, 56

Watermelon gazpacho shooters, *40*, 41

Whiskey:

digestivo, 199

sunny Irishman, 194

White bean:

and duck sausage cassoulet, 112–13, *113*

grilled chicken, and basil chili, 111

White chocolate risotto with orange ganache, 156–57, *157*

Wicked tea, 185, *185*

Wine, 177. *See also* Champagne; Prosecco

black sangria, 192

blush sangria, 192

buying guide, 211, 212

chilling, 145, 181

matching with food, 215

Merlot reduction, braised short ribs with, 100

-soaked figs and goat cheese, 46

Wonton(s):

crisps, seared ahi on, *32*, *33*

red curry chicken, with plum sauce, *22*, *23*

Workspace organization, 29

Y

Yogurt:

cucumber sauce, 102

harissa, 80

For Nate
who had better not grow up to be a picky eater!

Originally published in 2007 by Stewart, Tabori & Chang,
an imprint of Harry N. Abrams, Inc.

First paperback edition 2011
ISBN 978-1-57284-123-9

The Library of Congress has cataloged the hard cover editon of this book as follows:

Library of Congress Cataloging-in-Publication Data:
Smith, Dan, 1962
Talk with your mouth full : the Hearty Boys cookbook / Dan Smith and
Steve McDonagh ; photographs by Laurie Proffitt.
p. cm.
ISBN 978-1-58479-640-4
1. Cookery. 2. Entertaining. 3. Menus. I. McDonagh, Steve, 1964 II. Title.
TX714S58865 2007
641.5–dc22
2007009567

Thanks to the following vendors for their efforts:
A New Leaf Gardens and Studio (www.anewleafchicago.com)
BBJ Linen (www.bbjlinen.com)
Halls Rental (www.hallsrental.com)
Les Ruttenberg from Sams Wines and Liquors (www.samswine.com)
Rodrigo del Canto
Editor: Ann Treistman
Designer: Susi Oberhelman
Production Manager: Jacquie Poirier

The text of this book was composed in Dante and Avenir

Printed and bound in China

10 9 8 7 6 5 4 3 2 1

Surrey Books is an imprint of Agate Publishing. Agate books are available in bulk at
discount prices. For more information, go to agatepublishing.com.